The New Testament Books Made SIMPLE

Everything You Should
Have Learned
in Sunday School
(and Probably Didn't)

James E. Smith

Copyright © 2009
James E. Smith
All Rights Reserved

Unless otherwise noted, Scripture quotations are taken from THE HOLY BIBLE, NEW INTERNATIONAL VERSION®. NIV®. Copyright © 1973, 1978, 1984, by International Bible Society. Used by permission of Zondervan Publishing House. All rights reserved.

International Standard Book Number: 978-0-89900-990-2

Dedicated to
Grady and Irma Blevins
Dedicated Kingdom Workers
Friends in Christ

CONTENTS

1. Touring the New Testament Library   9

Section One
Foundation Books

2. Foundation Books (1)   23
   (Matthew & Mark)

3. Foundation Books (2)   35
   (Luke & John)

Section Two
Framework Book

4. Luke's Second Volume   47
   (Acts)

Section Three
Faith Books

Congregational Letters

5. Evangelical Epistles   57
   (Romans & Galatians)

6. Encounter Epistles   71
   (1 & 2 Corinthians)

7. Ecclesia Epistles   81
   (Ephesians, Philippians, Colossians)

8. Eschatological Epistles   97
   (1 & 2 Thessalonians)

Personal Letters

9. Letters to a Preacher   107
   (1 & 2 Timothy)

10. Letters to an Associate and a Friend   119
    (Titus & Philemon)

Section Four
Focus Books
Current Issues

11.	Jewish Christian Letters (Hebrews & James)	131
12.	Letters from an Apostle & a Brother (1 & 2 Peter, Jude)	143
13.	A Letter & Two Postcards (1, 2 & 3 John)	157

Future Issues

14.	Patmos Visions (Revelation)	169

PREFACE

This is the third volume of the *Made Simple* series. It has been my concern in this series to make basic information about the Bible as simple as it can be made. I intend this material for those who are Sunday School "dropouts," or those who never had the advantage of attending a congregation that stressed knowing God's Word.

In *Bible History Made Simple* I surveyed seventeen time zones of biblical history. Familiarity with the biblical timeline is the place to start in order to gain a mastery of the Bible. In volume two of this series we looked at the Old Testament library. We assessed the role of each book of that collection in the sacred symphony that is God's Word.

Now we undertake a similar investigation of the New Testament library. As in *Old Testament Books Made Simple* for each book I have followed an outline based on the boy Samuel's reply to God's voice: *Speak, for your servant hears* (1 Samuel 3:10). The letters of SPEAK will be an acronym to outline introductory material: S = situation; P = plan, i.e., how the book is structured; E = eternal purpose; A = acclaim for Jesus; K = keys. Under the heading HEAR outstanding chapters and verses in each book are suggested.

I have organized the study of the New Testament books into fourteen chapters. Chapter one is an overview of the entire content of the New Testament library. In the other thirteen chapters I have grouped the New Testament books. For the most part I have followed the order of the books as they appear in the English New Testament. I have departed from that order at two points. I deal with Romans and Galatians in one chapter. These two books belong together for both chronological and content reasons. For similar reasons I have placed the little book of Jude out of order with the two letters of Peter.

I do not intend for a class to cover an entire chapter of this guide in one week's lesson. My own teaching style puts emphasis on a Bible book each week. Certainly that seems appropriate for the larger New Testament books. Teachers may elect to combine some of the smaller books for a week's study.

Reading study guides is no substitute for getting into the Word itself. Students who are serious about this course will have as their goal reading through the books of the New Testament, keeping pace with the week-by-week class schedule. If time does not permit such an ambitious goal, at least read through the chapters suggested under the HEAR section of the larger books.

Christians believe that the New Testament is God's final revelation to the people of this world. It contains commands to obey, promises to believe, warnings to heed, and encouragement to uplift. From these pages we learn how "to do" church, evangelize the lost, and build up the body of Christ.

As you undertake this study, you may rest assured that my prayers are with you. May the Holy Spirit use these simple pages to guide you into a greater appreciation of this precious gift that we call the New Testament.

Pronouncing guide for some of the more difficult names has been adapted from Holman Bible Dictionary.

James E. Smith
Florida Christian College

Chapter One

Touring the New Testament Library

The Bible can be likened to a library of books housed in two separate buildings. The first building contains the earlier collection of books that Christians call the Old Testament. This collection was recognized as Scripture and preserved through tumult and trial by the Jewish nation. Part of Christian teaching is that God delivered to the Jews his oracles—his holy word—for safekeeping (Romans 3:2). For this reason Christians accept these earlier books as part of their Bible.

The second building of the biblical library houses the books of the New Testament. These books were written by leaders of the Christian community. They were recognized as Scripture and preserved by Christian congregations in various parts of the Roman Empire.

The space between the two buildings of the biblical library represents roughly four hundred years. This period is known as the Silent Period because God did not speak to his people. No prophets arose. No Scripture was written.

Contrasts in Collections

As we begin our tour of the New Testament library, we notice immediately four obvious contrasts between these newer books and those we observed on our tour of the earlier collection. First, there is a contrast in the number of books in each collection. As we count them in the English Bible, there are thirty-nine books in the Old Testament, only twenty-seven in the New. Second, there is a contrast in the time of writing. It took a thousand years—from Moses to Malachi—to complete the writing of the Old Testament. The New Testament books were all written over a period of only fifty years. Third, there is a contrast in the number of writers. About thirty-two writers contributed to the older collection, only eight or nine to the newer collection. Fourth, there is a contrast in the types of literature in the two collections. The Old Testament consists of books of law, history, poetry, and prophecy. In the New Testament the predominant type of literature is the epistle or letter.

How the Collection Grew

Most of the New Testament books were written to or for Christians in a specific congregation or region. As time went on the believers in other congregations made copies of these books. Still later the Christians began to publish manuscripts with collections of the books that they acknowledged to have been written by apostles or their representatives.

How the Collections Are Related

For the present it is important to grasp the overall message of the New Testament and how it relates to the message of the previous thirty-nine books. In our previous study (*Old Testament Books Made Simple*) we learned that the Old Testament was chapter one of the biblical story that might be entitled: *Christ is coming*. Chapter Two of that story is contained in the first four books of the New Testament: *Christ is here!* The rest of the books of the New Testament constitute the final chapter of that story: *Christ is coming again!*

Touring the Library

Organization of the Collection

The early New Testament manuscripts present a variety of arrangements of the books. Sections of the New Testament library have not always been in their present sequence. For example, the General Epistles precede Paul's epistles in some manuscripts. Even the individual books within sections have not always been placed in the same sequence. The arrangement of our English New Testament, however, represents what came to be the generally accepted order of the books.

In our previous study of the Old Testament we discovered that the thirty-nine Old Testament books are organized into shelves that can be labeled as follows:

- **Foundation Books** (Genesis–Deuteronomy)
- **Framework Books** (Joshua–Esther)
- **Faith Books** (Job–Song)
- **Focus Books**
  1. **Major Prophets** (Isaiah–Daniel)
  2. **Minor Prophets** (Hosea–Malachi)

The New Testament library is organized in a similar manner:

- **Foundation Books (Matthew–John)**
- **Framework Book (Acts)**
- **Faith Books (Romans–Philemon)**
- **Focus Books**
  1. **Focus on current issues** (Hebrews–Jude)
  2. **Focus on future issues** (Revelation)

A Closer Look at the Shelves

Foundation Books

The Foundation Books of the New Testament are the four Gospels: Matthew, Mark, Luke, and John. These books are called

Gospels because they contain the good news of the birth, ministry, death, burial, resurrection, and ascension of Jesus Christ. The four Gospels function in the New Testament in a manner similar to the first five books of the Old Testament. They are foundational to everything else that is recorded in the books that follow. The Gospels record the basic factual information about the life of Christ including his teaching on various subjects.

Framework Book

It took twelve books in the Old Testament to provide the framework for the thousand years that elapsed between Moses and Malachi. The New Testament is concerned about less than one tenth of that amount of time. From the ascension of Jesus to the death of the Apostle John is a period of about seventy years. The Book of Acts is the only Framework Book in the New Testament. It does not contain a complete framework for the New Testament period. Acts covers only about thirty-five years (one half) of the years of New Testament history. The second half of New Testament history must be reconstructed from hints given in the later epistles, the Book of Revelation, and early secular and Christian historians.

Faith Books

In *Old Testament Books Made Simple* we used "Faith Books" as the designation for the five books of Job, Psalms, Proverbs, Ecclesiastes, and Song of Solomon. These books explored how faith in God responds to the varied circumstances of life. In the New Testament we use "Faith Books" with a different connotation. The New Testament Faith Books are the letters of Paul. Some have referred to Paul as the first Christian theologian and the architect of the Christian faith. If such designations imply that Christianity owes its existence to the genius of Paul, then they misrepresent his role. It is true, however, that in the oral and written teaching of Paul the contours of the Christian faith were drawn by the Holy Spirit. In the writings of Paul above all other New Testament writers, the Christian faith was defined and refined.

Touring the Library

In our English Bibles the letters of Paul are divided into two broad groups: public letters and private letters. The former group is arranged according to size:

Paul's Letters as Arranged in Our Bibles	
Public Letters	**Private Letters**
Romans 1 Corinthians 2 Corinthians Galatians Ephesians Philippians Colossians 1 Thessalonians 2 Thessalonians	1 Timothy 2 Timothy Titus Philemon
Written to 7 Churches	**Written to 3 Individuals**

The public letters were written to congregations. They were intended to be read as part of the Christian assembly.

If Paul's letters were to appear in our Bibles in the order in which they were written the layout would look like what is presented in the following chart.

Paul's Letters Chronologically Grouped			
2nd Journey Letters	**3rd Journey Letters**	**Prison Period Letters**	**Final Letters**
1 Thessalonians 2 Thessalonians	Galatians Romans 1 Corinthians 2 Corinthians	Colossians Philemon Philippians Ephesians	1 Timothy Titus Hebrews (?) 2 Timothy

In this survey we will look at Paul's letters in the order in which they appear in the English Bible with one exception. We will consider Galatians along with Romans because of the similarity of content. Here is the organization of Paul's letters utilized in this survey:

❖ **Evangelical Duo** (Romans & Galatians)
❖ **Encounter Duo** (1 & 2 Corinthians)

13

- ❖ **Ecclesia Trio** (Ephesians–Colossians)
- ❖ **Eschatological Duo** (1 & 2 Thessalonians)
- ❖ **Exhortation Quartet** (1 Timothy–Philemon)

Focus Books

The Old Testament Focus Books had two distinct subdivisions: Major Prophets and Minor Prophets. Likewise, the section of New Testament Focus Books has two subdivisions. The first subdivision consists of eight open letters that focus on specific issues that were of concern to the entire Christian community. Frequently New Testament scholars refer to these eight books as the ***General Epistles***.

The eight General Epistles were written by five men. The authorship of Hebrews is uncertain. The position of the Book of Hebrews immediately following the collection of letters by Paul reflects the ambiguity of authorship of this particular book. Some regard Hebrews as the fourteenth book written by Paul. Others are content to attribute Hebrews to some unknown Christian teacher. James and Jude were the half brothers of Jesus. Three of the General Epistles were written by John the beloved disciple. Two were penned by the Apostle Peter.

The second subdivision of the New Testament Focus Books consists of one volume—Revelation. John's fifth contribution to the New Testament library is unique in the collection. While it contains brief letters to seven churches, it focuses mainly on issues pertaining to the near and the distant future.

Observations about Writers

A quick stroll through the New Testament library produces some initial impressions about the contents of this collection of books in terms of authorship and date of the individual volumes.

A. Original Apostles Who Wrote

We first notice that the majority of the New Testament books were written by those who were apostles of Jesus Christ. The word *apostle* means one who has been sent out on behalf of another. The word, however, has a technical sense in the New Testament. It is used of one of the men chosen by Christ to be an official eyewitness of his resurrection. With the exception of Paul, who was a special case, these men had traveled with Jesus from the beginning of his ministry. They had been with him 24/7 for the better part of three and a half years. Thus they could authoritatively testify that the same Jesus who died on the cross was the Jesus who appeared to them and other disciples over the course of forty days prior to his ascension.

The **Apostle John** wrote five books of the New Testament — the Gospel of John, the letter called 1 John, two postcards called 2 & 3 John, and the Book of Revelation. All together this material constitutes about eighteen percent of the New Testament text.

The **Apostle Peter** wrote two short letters. He may also have influenced the contents of the Gospel of Mark.

The **Apostle Matthew** wrote a Gospel. This large book constitutes about twelve percent of the New Testament text.

B. Apostle to the Gentiles

Paul was the last apostle to be named. He came from the ranks of those who hated Christ and his followers. In the fourth year of the history of the church Saul (as he was then called) was making a trip to Damascus to ferret out the Christians from the synagogues. He aimed to return them to Jerusalem for trial and execution. About noon he saw a blinding light. A voice from heaven identifying himself as Jesus directed Paul to go into Damascus. There he was to be given further instructions.

Paul had no doubt that he had both seen and heard the resurrected Christ on the Damascus road. Without question he came to believe in Christ. He repented of his vicious attacks on the Christians. In darkness he prayed for forgiveness and waited for the further instructions promised by the voice on the road.

Three days later the Lord dispatched a local Christian named Ananias to minister to Paul. First, Ananias restored Paul's eyesight. Then he exhorted the man to be baptized. Finally, Ananias told Paul that he was to be a light to the Gentiles.

Immediately following his baptism Paul began to preach the truth about Christ in the Jewish synagogues of Damascus. Clearly this anti-Christian persecutor was now a fervent Christian. The only possible explanation for such a sudden and complete turnabout in this man's life is that on the Damascus road he actually had seen the resurrected Jesus in his heavenly glory.

Both bookwise and wordwise Paul contributed more to the New Testament than any other writer. He wrote the thirteen books designated above as Faith Books. The Book of Hebrews is anonymous. Ancient tradition assigned the book to various authors, but the tradition that the book was written by Paul is very strong. If Hebrews is assigned to Paul, than the Apostle to the Gentiles wrote half the books of the New Testament and about twenty-eight percent of the actual text.

C. Non-Apostles Who Wrote

Four non-Apostles also contributed to the New Testament library: Luke, Mark, James, and Jude. **Luke**, the Gentile traveling companion of Paul, wrote two large books of the New Testament—the Gospel of Luke and the Book of Acts. Together these two books contain only ten fewer words than the combined epistles of Paul (Hebrews included). So Luke contributed about twenty-eight percent of the New Testament text.

Christian tradition indicates that **Mark** wrote his Gospel while in Rome working alongside of Peter. The early Christians considered Mark's Gospel to be virtually the memoirs of the great Apostle Peter.

The writer of the Book of **James** was not the Apostle James, the brother of John. Rather he was the brother of Jesus. The brothers were nonbelievers during Jesus' ministry. After his resurrection Jesus made a special one-on-one appearance to James (1 Corinthians 15:7). Thereafter James became one of the most influential leaders in the early church.

Jude (short for Judas) identifies himself as *the brother of James*. This means that two of the New Testament books were written by half brothers of Jesus.

The following chart summarizes the above data:

New Testament Writers		
Name	Books	Text percent
Paul	13 or 14	27.8%
Luke	2	27.8%
John	5	18.9%
Matthew	1	13.1%
Mark	1	8.4%
Peter	2	2.4%
James	1	1.3%
Jude	1	.3%
Eight Writers	27 Books	100%

Observations about the Time of Writing

According to some New Testament authorities, the earliest New Testament book was **James** (AD 48). This means that the early Christians met for worship for eighteen years before any part of the New Testament was available in written form for their study. They did have, however, the **apostles** who were guided by the Holy Spirit into all truth. The apostles recited the teachings of Jesus and taught the new truths that the Holy Spirit revealed to them.

In many congregations there were also **prophets**. These were people who received special revelations from God to share with the local brethren. The oral teaching of the apostles and prophets served the needs of the church until such time as the books of the New Testament began to be written.

Many think Mark is the earliest Gospel because it is the shortest. Ancient Christian tradition, however, regards **Matthew** (AD

50) as the earliest Gospel. That is why Matthew stands first in most New Testament manuscripts. Luke's Gospel can be assigned to about the year AD 58, and Mark to about AD 68.

There is some dispute about which of Paul's epistles is the earliest. Some think Galatians was the first letter Paul penned. A better case, however, can be made for designating **1 & 2 Thessalonians** (AD 50–51) as the apostle's earliest correspondence. The last letter Paul wrote was 2 Timothy. He wrote this letter just before his death in AD 68. So the writings of Paul span a period of about eighteen years.

The most prolific period for writing New Testament books was the **decade of the sixties**. Twelve books were written between the years AD 60–69.

The General Epistles are very difficult to date. The same is true of Revelation. Most date Revelation to about AD 90. Others think that the book was written before the fall of Jerusalem in AD 70.

The following chart displays the approximate dates for the New Testament books:

	New Testament Books according to Date
AD 40–49	James (48)
AD 50–59	Matthew (50); 1 Thessalonians (50); 2 Thessalonians (51); 1 Corinthians (55); 2 Corinthians (55); Galatians (55); Romans (56); Luke (58)
AD 60–69	Acts (61); Colossians (63); Philemon (63); Ephesians (63); Philippians (63); 1 Peter (65); 2 Peter (67); 1 Timothy (67); Titus (67); 2 Timothy (68); Mark (68); Hebrews (68)
AD 70–79	Jude (75)
AD 90–96	Gospel of John (90); 1 John (90); 2 John (90); 3 John (90); Revelation (90)

We have now completed our whirlwind tour of the New Testament library. We have learned some fundamental facts about this wonderful collection of writings that for Christians is the final authority for matters of faith. We have learned that the New Testament is a collection of . . .

Touring the Library

❖ **27 books**
❖ **By at least 8 human authors**
❖ **Written over a period of about 50 years**
❖ **Organized in 4 shelves**

Now it's time to go back and look at these books more closely. So let's get started!

Section One

FOUNDATION BOOKS

Matthew

Mark

Luke

John

Chapter Two

FOUNDATION BOOKS (1)
Matthew–Mark

Matthew, Mark, and Luke are called the **synoptic gospels**. *Synoptic* means *taking a common or similar view*. There is a great deal of overlap in these three Gospels; but each arranges the material and tells the story from a particular point of view and for a particular audience. In this chapter we will survey the first two of the Gospels.

40th Book of the Bible
Gospel of Matthew
The Jewish Gospel

The name *Matthew* means *gift of God*. The author was also known by the name *Levi*. Matthew was *the son of Alphaeus* (Mark 2:14). He had a brother named James who was also chosen by Jesus as an apostle (Matthew 10:3; Mark 3:18; Luke 6:15; Acts 1:13). His mother may have been one of several women named Mary in the New Testament. She kept vigil at the foot of the cross with the mother of Jesus (Matthew 27:55-56; Mark 15:40).

Before his call to discipleship, Matthew was a tax collector. His tax booth was located at Capernaum on the main north-south highway from Damascus to Egypt. Matthew's duty was to collect "toll" or "transport" taxes from locals carrying their goods to market as well as from long-distance caravans. He was an employee of Herod Antipas who ruled Galilee as a Tetrarch appointed by Rome. A *Tetrarch* was a king of sorts who ruled a small territory subject to oversight of Roman authorities.

Legend has it that during the early years of the church Matthew traveled to Ethiopia. There he became associated with Candace, identified with the eunuch of Acts 8:27. The legend goes on to relate that Matthew died a martyr's death in Ethiopia.

Matthew was well qualified to pen the earliest Gospel. First, by training he must have been a meticulous record keeper. He was also an apostle of Jesus. He was therefore an eyewitness of most of the events that he reports in his Gospel.

Matthew's Gospel contains twenty-eight chapters, 1,071 verses, and 23,684 words. These statistics make Matthew the third largest book of the New Testament.

Situation

Matthew's Gospel dates to about AD 50. By the year AD 50 the church had survived twenty years without any official or inspired record of the life of her Lord. Most of those who made up the church at this time were of Jewish background. Matthew determined to provide for these believers a teaching manual and an evangelistic tool.

That Matthew had a Jewish target audience is indicated by the content of the book. First, Jews were interested in the Old Testament predictions concerning the Messiah. In the first Gospel Jesus declared that twenty-one prophecies had been fulfilled. Matthew himself pointed out another twenty-one predictions fulfilled in the events of the life of Christ. None of the other Gospels comes close to this number of fulfillment claims.

Second, Jews held the Law of Moses in great respect. They were concerned about the attitude of Jesus toward the Law. Matthew's Gospel contains many positive statements that Jesus made regarding the Law of Moses.

Third, every religious Jew knew that the Messiah had to come from the line of David. Matthew takes pains to trace the legal ancestry of Jesus (through Joseph his legal father) back to David.

Fourth, Jews were expecting God to establish a glorious kingdom on earth. Matthew mentioned the kingdom fifty-six times, more than any of the other three Gospels.

Plan

The Gospel of Matthew contains sermons and parables of Jesus as well as a narrative account of his ministry. This material is organized in a most orderly format. The former tax collector displays organizational genius. This is especially evident in the way he handles the genealogy of Jesus (1:17) and the account of Jesus' temptation (4:1, 11).

Structural plan. The key word in the structure of Matthew is the word *finished* (7:28; 11:1; 13:53; 19:1; 26:1). The Gospel is easily divided into seven sections: a beginning and an end with five teaching sections between. These sections of teaching are: 1) the Sermon on the Mount (chs. 5–7); 2) commissioning of the Twelve (ch. 10); 3) sermon by the sea (ch. 13); 4) guidelines for kingdom citizens (ch. 18); and 5) warnings about the end of the age (chs. 24–25). Thus Matthew appears to highlight the teaching ministry of Jesus.

The following outline of Matthew's Gospel is appealing because it brings out the book's emphasis on Jesus' royalty:

- ❖ **Preparation for the King** (1:1–4:11)
- ❖ **Principles of the King** (4:12–7:29)
- ❖ **Power of the King** (8:1–10:42)
- ❖ **Program of the King** (11:1–13:52)
- ❖ **Purpose of the King** (13:53–18:35)
- ❖ **Problems of the King** (19:1–25:46)
- ❖ **Passion of the King** (26:1–28:20)

Geographical plan. The story of Jesus unfolds in what is now Israel. His ministry took place largely in the northern part of the land around the **Sea of Galilee**. Jesus, however, made several trips to **Jerusalem** in the region of Judea. He also ministered briefly in **Samaria** (the region between Galilee and Judea) and in **Perea** east of the Jordan River. Geographically the material in Matthew falls into four divisions:

- ❖ **Galilee and Judea** (1:1–4:11)
- ❖ **Galilee** (4:12–18:35)
- ❖ **Perea and Judea** (19:1–25:46)
- ❖ **Judea and Galilee** (26:1–28:20)

Chronological plan. Matthew begins with Jesus' birth about 5 BC and concludes with his final commission to his disciples in AD 30. The book covers about thirty-five years, with primary emphasis on the 3.5 years of Jesus' ministry.

Biographical plan. Of course the focus of this Gospel is on Jesus. Matthew shows that the carpenter who became an itinerant preacher is truly the Jewish Messiah and our Savior. Among the disciples, clearly Matthew highlights *Peter*. He was the vocal and impulsive leader of the Twelve. Jesus' antagonists throughout the book are the Pharisees. They were zealous legalists who stressed the traditions of the Jewish elders even at the expense of the plain teaching of the word of God.

Eternal Purpose

The immediate purpose of the Gospel of Matthew is to provide a topical account of the life of Christ for the Jewish Christian community of Syria-Palestine. The ultimate purpose of the book is to demonstrate that Jesus of Nazareth is the Messiah promised throughout the Old Testament.

Matthew brackets his entire account between two key thesis statements. In Christ God was uniquely present with us in the flesh (1:23). He will be with us to the end of the present age (28:20). Matthew reinforces his brackets with a supporting thought in 18:20. Jesus continues to be with us whenever two or three gather in his name.

Clearly Matthew had an instructional purpose in writing his Gospel. He systematically presents the claims, credentials, ethical and theological teachings of the Lord Jesus. For this reason Matthew has been used as a teaching manual since the early years of the church.

Acclaim

Matthew paints a portrait of Jesus as the **Promised Sovereign**. The word *promised* refers to Matthew's abundant citation of Old Testament predictions. He saw Jesus as the fulfillment of centuries of Jewish longing for a Messiah (*Anointed One*) — a Prophet, Priest, and King par excellence. The word *Sovereign* refers to Jesus' kingly office. It is this office that is especially highlighted by Matthew. Yet Jesus distanced himself from current notions of a physical, earthly, material throne and reign. Matthew's account begins with the search for a king (2:2). In Jesus' final teaching parable, one recorded only by Matthew, he portrays himself as a King at the final judgment (25:31-46). At the end of Jesus' life Matthew records the mockery of his claim to kingship (27:42).

Keys

The key chapter in the Gospel of Matthew is chapter 12. In this chapter the religious leaders formally reject Jesus' claims to be the Messiah.

The key verse in the book is this: *Repent, for the kingdom of heaven is near* (Matthew 3:2). One could also make an argument that the key verses are 16:16-19 (Peter's great confession) or 28:18-20 (the Great Commission).

Key phrases in the book include *kingdom of heaven* (33) and *might be/was fulfilled* (9).

Key words include *king* (20) and *blessed* (18).

Special Features

Some interesting facts about the Gospel of Matthew that make it stand out in the sacred collection are these:

- ❖ According to ancient authorities, Matthew was originally written in the Hebrew language. If so, it was very

early translated into Greek. The oldest manuscripts that we have of Matthew are in Greek.
- ❖ From the earliest days this Gospel was the most widely read and in some respects the most influential of the four Gospels.
- ❖ Matthew contains the most complete record of what Jesus taught. Fully sixty percent of 1,071 verses in this Gospel contain the spoken word of Jesus.
- ❖ More than any of the other Gospels, Matthew quotes the Old Testament—at least fifty-seven times, compared with thirty in the runner-up, Mark.
- ❖ In Christian symbolism Matthew is represented by a lion.
- ❖ Matthew is the only Gospel to mention the church (16:18; 18:17).
- ❖ Matthew's narrative material is more concise than the parallel narratives in the other Gospels.
- ❖ Matthew records ten parables not recorded in the other Gospels.
- ❖ Matthew records three miracles not recorded elsewhere: the two blind men (9:27-31); the dumb demoniac (9:32-33); the coin in the fish's mouth (17:24-27).
- ❖ In the teaching of Jesus Matthew emphasizes the kingdom of heaven. He points out repeatedly that Christ's kingdom will include Gentiles as well as Jews.

HEAR

Through Matthew's Gospel God has spoken. We, like Samuel of old, must hear the message. From those passages that are unique to the Gospel of Matthew, here are some of the outstanding chapters:

- ❖ Jesus' birth and visit of Magi (Matthew 1–2)
- ❖ Sermon on the Mount (Matthew 5–7)
- ❖ Parables: weeds, treasure, and pearl (Matthew 13)
- ❖ Peter's great confession (Matthew 16)

- ❖ Several details about Jesus' crucifixion and resurrection are unique to Matthew (Matthew 27-28)
- ❖ Parables of ten virgins and the talents (Matthew 25)

Here are some favorite lines from the first Gospel:
- ❖ *Do to others what you would have them do to you* (7:12). The Golden Rule.
- ❖ *Man does not live on bread alone* (4:4). A quotation from Deuteronomy.
- ❖ *Blessed are the meek, for they will inherit the earth* (5:5).
- ❖ *Therefore go and make disciples of all nations, baptizing them in the name of the Father and of the Son and of the Holy Spirit* (28:19).

41st Book of the Bible
Gospel of Mark
The Roman Gospel

The author's full name was John Mark. He is mentioned eight times in the rest of the New Testament. *John* is the shortened form of a Hebrew name meaning *Yahweh has shown grace*. *Mark* is a shortened form of *Marcus*, a Latin name. It was not uncommon for first-century Jews to have a Greek or Roman name in addition to their Hebrew name.

Mark's father is never mentioned. His mother was one of several New Testament women named *Mary*. She was a wealthy Christian who lived in a large house in Jerusalem (Acts 12:12). Mary was related to Barnabas (Colossians 4:10).

What direct association Mark had with Jesus, if any, is not stated in the Gospels. An early Christian writer says that Mark "was neither a hearer nor a companion of the Lord." Many think, however, that Mark was the anonymous young man of Mark 14:51, who saved himself from arrest in the Garden by fleeing naked.

Mark rubbed elbows with the greatest leaders in the early church. He was a companion of Paul and Barnabas on their first missionary journey. He accompanied Barnabas on the second

Cyprus campaign (Acts 15:39). Mark was an associate of Peter in Rome (1 Peter 5:13). He was with Paul during his first Roman imprisonment (Colossians 4:10). In Philemon 24 Mark is associated with Luke. He was working with Timothy in ministry when Paul sent for him (2 Timothy 4:11).

The Book of Mark contains sixteen chapters, 678 verses, and 15,171 words.

Situation

Mark was published shortly after the death of Peter about AD 68. As Peter began to age, Mark became concerned about recording his recollections concerning the events in Christ's life. The earliest statement about the origin of the second Gospel describes Mark as "the interpreter of Peter." The same source says that Mark wrote down accurately all that Peter remembered, whether of sayings or deeds of Christ, but not in order.

Since Mark was working in Rome at the time he compiled his Gospel, it is reasonable to assume that he wrote primarily for Romans. This assumption is supported by six pieces of evidence. First, the size of the second Gospel is what would appeal to the Roman mind. They were not a people who were given to flowery literary composition. Second, Mark emphasizes the deeds of Jesus. He records nineteen miracles in the sixteen chapters of the book. Romans were people who appreciated power and action.

Third, the refrain *straightway* (KJV) or *immediately* (NIV) is used thirty-six times by Mark. This presents a picture of Jesus constantly on the go. He is busy, busy, busy. This picture would appeal to the energetic Romans. Fourth, Mark contains few references to the Old Testament. One would hardly expect Romans to appreciate the significance of prophetic fulfillment. Fifth, on occasion Mark uses Latin terms. At times he interjects parenthetical explanations of Jewish phrases and customs, of Israel's geography and of Aramaic words that would be familiar to natives of Palestine (e.g., 7:3). These explanations suggest that he was writing for an audience far removed from Palestine. Finally, Mark gives prominence to Gentiles in his Gospel (11:17; 13:10; 14:9).

Plan

Mark's Gospel does not indicate the careful arrangement of either Matthew or Luke. Mark aimed to produce an action-packed account of Jesus' life such as would appeal to red-blooded Romans. His account jumps from one miracle of Jesus to another, and from one confrontation to another. In this Gospel Jesus silences demons, feeds thousands, calms storms, walks on water, endures suffering heroically, and dies only to rise from the dead.

Mark uses the Greek present tense 151 times to depict action in progress. He thereby draws his readers into the scenes he sketches. Though more selective in the episodes he includes, Mark's vivid descriptions are often more detailed than the parallel accounts in the other Gospels. Mark's vigorous and blunt Greek reflects the language of the common man. For this reason the Gospel of Mark is the favorite of many, especially men.

Structural plan. The second Gospel puts the emphasis on the ministry of God's Servant Jesus. The book has two main divisions with an appropriate introduction and conclusion. The outline of Mark looks like this:

- ❖ **Preparation for the Servant** (1:1-13)
- ❖ **Ministration of the Servant** (1:14-8:30)
- ❖ **Rejection of the Servant** (8:31-15:47)
- ❖ **Exaltation of the Servant** (ch. 16)

Chronological plan. The focus of Mark is narrower than that of Matthew. Mark says nothing of the birth of Jesus. Romans would not particularly be interested in birth stories. So the second Gospel covers only about 3.5 years—from Jesus' baptism to his ascension. Mark, however, does not appear to follow chronological sequence in the arrangement of his book. He seems to be more concerned about facilitating memorization of the material. Stories and sayings are linked by keywords or similarity of subject.

Biographical plan. Of course, Jesus is the star of the Gospel. The supporting cast is the Twelve. Mark mentions the Twelve Apostles more than any other Gospel.

Geographical plan. Mark is similar to Matthew. The first two Gospels focus on action that takes place mostly in Galilee and Jerusalem.

Eternal Purpose

The immediate purpose of the Gospel of Mark is to record for the believers in Rome the recollections of Peter as both a training manual and an evangelistic tool. The ultimate purpose of the book is to demonstrate that Jesus is the powerful servant of the Father.

The basic lesson taught in this book is that we must follow Jesus in the path of service.

Acclaim

Mark paints a portrait of Jesus as the **Powerful Servant**. His power was exhibited throughout his ministry in the numerous miracles Mark records.

Mark focuses on the deeds of Jesus more than his declarations. Because this is the story of God's Servant, Mark omits Jesus' ancestry and birth. He moves right into his public ministry. The way this Servant worked is a model for his followers. Jesus acted *wisely* in his selection of his close associates (1:14-20; 2:13-14; 3:14-19). He acted *authoritatively* in dealing with spiritual and natural forces (1:21-28; 4:35-41; 5:1-43; 6:47-51; 9:14-29). Jesus worked *compassionately* (1:29-34, 40-45), *prayerfully* (1:35; 6:46; 14:32-41), and *unselfishly* (3:20; 6:31). He also acted with *dignity* (11:1-33). Jesus faced his final confrontation with his adversaries *fearlessly* (chs. 14–15).

This Gospel presents a more detailed picture of the suffering of Jesus than do the other three Gospels. In the earlier chapters Mark highlights the pain Jesus endured in his confrontations with spiritual forces and hostile religious authorities. He even experienced rejection from his family and closest friends. The climax of his suffering, however, comes in the concluding chapters of Mark. Over one third of the material in Mark focuses on the last week of Jesus' life.

Keys

The key chapter in the Gospel of Mark is chapter 8. In this chapter Peter confesses Jesus as Christ. For his part, Christ begins to focus his ministry on preparing his disciples for what they will experience in Jerusalem within a few weeks. Prior to chapter 8 the focus is on Christ's service. Following chapter 8 the emphasis is on his sacrifice.

This twofold emphasis of Mark is captured in the key verse: *The Son of Man did not come to be served, but to serve, and to give his life as a ransom for many* (10:45).

The key phrases in the book include *in those days* (6) and *verily I say* (15 KJV).

The Key word in Mark is *straightway* or *immediately* (36).

Special Features

Some of the unusual features of the second Gospel that set it apart within the sacred collection are these:

- ❖ In the early days of the church Mark had the nickname *kolobodaktylos* = *stumpy-fingered*. This may refer either to a physical peculiarity on the part of the author or to some strange stylistic features of his Gospel.
- ❖ Mark's Gospel contains fewer teachings of Jesus than any other Gospel.
- ❖ In Christian symbolism Mark is represented by an ox, an animal that connotes service and sacrifice.
- ❖ Of the sixteen chapters in this book, six are devoted to the final week of Jesus' life.
- ❖ To reduce opposition until his mission was complete, Jesus repeatedly told people not to say anything about his identity or what miracles he had done.
- ❖ Jesus used parables as coded messages to his followers — messages hidden from his opponents (Mark 4:10-12).
- ❖ At least 601 of the 678 verses in Mark (89%) repeat verses from Matthew's Gospel.
- ❖ The oldest manuscripts conclude the Gospel of Mark with the women running from the tomb, too afraid to

tell anyone what they had discovered (Mark 16:8). The longer ending, familiar from the KJV, appears in the majority of manuscripts.
- ❖ The majority of Christian scholars regard Mark's Gospel as the earliest of the four primarily because it is the shortest.
- ❖ Mark records over half of Christ's thirty-five miracles, the highest proportion in the Gospels.

HEAR

To sample some of what Mark has to offer in his Gospel, read the following outstanding chapters:
- ❖ Call of the Twelve (Mark 3)
- ❖ Healing of the Gadarene demoniac (Mark 5)
- ❖ Jesus and the Phoenician woman (Mark 7)

Here are some famous lines from the Gospel of Mark:
- ❖ *Many who are first will be last, and the last first* (10:31).
- ❖ *I will make you fishers of men* (1:17).
- ❖ *Give to Caesar what is Caesar's and to God what is God's.* (12:17).

Chapter Three

FOUNDATION BOOKS (2)
Luke–John

The Gospel of Luke is the third of the Synoptic (seen together) Gospels. It contains much material in common with Matthew and Mark. In terms of the portrait of Christ, however, Luke is the flip side of John. For that reason these two Gospels are discussed together in this chapter.

42nd Book of the Bible
Gospel of Luke
The Greek Gospel

Luke is mentioned only three times in the New Testament. Paul refers to him as *the beloved physician* (Colossians 4:14) and one of his *fellow laborers* (Philemon 24). He no doubt ministered to Paul's personal medical needs on his second missionary journey, and during Paul's imprisonment in Rome. Luke also helped in the work of preaching the gospel. He was the first medical missionary. Some scholars think that Luke was the first minister of the church at Philippi. Just before Paul's execution by the emperor Nero, Luke is mentioned for the last time in the Bible. Paul says, *only Luke is with me* (2 Timothy 4:11).

Luke generally is thought to have been a Gentile. Early Christian tradition says that Luke came from Antioch of Syria, that he, like Paul, was single, and that he lived to the age of 84.

The Gospel of Luke was written for someone named *Theophilus*, which means *lover of God* (1:3). He probably was a wealthy Gentile Christian who provided the money to get the book of Luke published. It is thought that he lived in or near Rome. Luke wrote this book with Gentiles like Theophilus in mind.

The Gospel of Luke contains twenty-four chapters, 1,151 verses, and 25,944 words. It is the largest book in the New Testament.

Situation

The Gospel of Luke was written about AD 58. This was about eight years after Matthew, and about ten years before Mark wrote his Gospel. As noted above, Luke was a Gentile. He had ministered many years among the Gentiles. Luke saw the need for a Gospel that would appeal to the special interests of the intellectuals of society, the Greeks.

In the opening verses Luke asserts that there had been many attempts to write a record of the life of Christ. Because he was not an eyewitness of events in the life of Christ, Luke determined to use the techniques of an investigative reporter. As a missionary companion of the Apostle Paul, Luke traveled widely. No doubt he had access on numerous occasions to those who were intimate associates of Christ during his earthly ministry.

That Luke's intended audience was Greek is indicated by six characteristics of this Gospel. First, Luke wrote in polished Greek. That would appeal to Greek readers. Second, in this Gospel he shows the Greek interest in precise dates and marks of time. Third, this Gospel takes note of contemporary rulers not mentioned in the other Gospels. Fourth, Luke emphasizes the humanity of Jesus. He alone fulfills the Greek ideal of human perfection. His was the greatest life ever lived. Fifth, Luke traces Jesus' ancestry back, not just to Abraham, but to Adam. Thus he suggests that Jesus is a true son of man. The genealogy testifies that he belongs as much to Gentiles as to Jews. Finally, Luke makes comparatively infrequent use of the Old Testament.

Plan

The third Gospel contains an abundance of narrative. It has more parables that any other Gospel. It also includes a genealogy and some songs of praise.

Structural plan. The Gospel of Luke is organized in three main sections that can be labeled as follows:

- ❖ **Preparation for Ministry** (1:1–4:13)
- ❖ **Participation in Ministry** (4:14–19:27)
- ❖ **Pinnacle of Ministry** (19:28–24:53)

Biographical plan. The focus obviously is on Jesus. He is presented as both Son of Man and Son of God. Luke also emphasizes the role of the Twelve Apostles in Jesus' ministry.

Luke was a people person. He paints unforgettable portraits of characters like Zechariah (*zehk-uh-ri'-uh*), the Good Samaritan, the Prodigal Son, the little tax collector Zaccheus (*zak-kee'-uhs*), and the two disciples on the Emmaus road.

Geographical plan. The main center of Jesus' ministry is in Galilee. Luke records his visitations to the regions of Samaria, Decapolis, Judea, and Perea (beyond Jordan) as well.

Eternal Purpose

Luke states his purpose in this note to Theophilus (*thi-ahf'-ih-luhs*): *so that you may know the certainty of the things you have been taught* (1:4). Theophilus already was a believer; but he was in need of further grounding in the truth about Jesus. Many false teachers were twisting the facts of Christ's life. Theophilus needed to have accurate facts upon which to build his faith.

The immediate purpose of the Gospel of Luke is to present to the Gentile Christian community an accurate record of the life of Christ to replace the partial and less reliable accounts that were circulating widely in Gentile churches. The ultimate purpose of this book is to show the human side of Jesus—his compassion and tenderness—with all classes of society.

Luke's aim may have been threefold: pastoral, evangelistic, and legal. On the **pastoral level** he intended his reliable record of Christ's life to strengthen the faith of Gentile Christians. Luke was a missionary at heart. On the **evangelistic** level Luke aimed to present facts that would draw Gentiles to Christ intellectually and emotionally as well. Luke may have written this Gospel during the two years Paul was in Roman custody in Caesarea. He may have intended this Gospel to serve as a **legal** response to the false accusations that Christianity was politically a subversive sect.

The underlying premise of this Gospel is that Jesus is the Savior of the human race. Every event, miracle, and teaching points to this great truth. Early in the narrative the angels reveal to shepherds: *Today in the town of David a Savior has been born to you; he is Christ the Lord* (2:11).

Luke's thesis that Christ is the Savior of all men is reinforced in several ways. Luke cites the Old Testament that Gentiles will receive the light of divine revelation (2:32; 3:6). The parable of the Good Samaritan puts a despised race in a positive light. For Luke the Son of Man is the Savior for all men: Jews, Samaritans, Gentiles; poor and rich; respectable and despised; tax collectors and religious leaders; women and children.

Acclaim

Luke's Gospel paints the portrait of Jesus as the ***Son of Man***. This writer stresses the humanity and compassion of Jesus. Luke gives the most complete account of Christ's ancestry, and birth. Only in Luke is Jesus pictured passing through the various stages of human existence (2:51-52). He is the perfect Son of Man. Jesus identified with the sorrow and plight of sinful men so that he might carry our sorrows and offer us salvation. Luke mentions more prayers of Jesus than the other Gospel writers. He notes the tears of Jesus over the city of Jerusalem (19:41). In this Gospel Jesus interacts more with women and children than in the others.

Keys

The key chapter in the Gospel of Luke is chapter 15. This chapter captures the special thrust of this Gospel in the parables of the lost sheep, the lost coin, and the lost son.

The key verse in the book is this: *The Son of Man came to seek and to save what was lost* (19:10).

The key word in the book is *salvation/savior* (8).

Special Features

Like every book in the Bible, the Gospel of Luke has some distinctive features. These include the following:

- ❖ Luke followed up his Gospel with a sequel—the Book of Acts.
- ❖ Luke employed the technique of an investigative reporter in compiling his Gospel (Luke 1:1-4).
- ❖ Luke offers the most comprehensive account of the life of Christ.
- ❖ Luke refers to Jesus with the Greek term *teacher* rather than the Jewish term *rabbi*.
- ❖ Luke was the only non-Jewish writer of Scripture.
- ❖ During a drought in Israel in 1986 the shoreline of the Sea of Galilee receded dramatically. Two men discovered in the mud an ancient fishing boat. The boat came from the time of Christ. The boat could hold at least fifteen men. Some have dubbed the find "the Jesus boat," thinking that this may have been the actual boat used by Jesus and the Twelve.
- ❖ Luke is the longest book of the New Testament.
- ❖ In Christian art Luke is represented by a man.

HEAR

God speaks in the Gospel of Luke. We would do well to listen. Some of the best-loved stories in the Bible are found in Luke. Fourteen of Jesus' parables are found only in this Gospel, as are

six of his miracles. Here are a few outstanding chapters that will introduce you to this Gospel:
- ❖ Shepherds discover the Christ child (Luke 2)
- ❖ The great gulf in the afterlife (Luke 16)
- ❖ The Good Samaritan (Luke 10)

Here are some famous lines from the Gospel of Luke:
- ❖ *Our Father which art in heaven, Hallowed be thy name* (11:2 KJV).
- ❖ *Glory to God in the highest, and on earth peace to him on whom his favor rests* (2:14).
- ❖ *Physician, heal yourself* (4:23).
- ❖ *I am sending you out like lambs among wolves* (10:3).

43rd Book of the Bible
Gospel of John
The Universal Gospel

John is usually assumed to be the youngest of the Twelve. He and his brother James were sons of Zebedee, a fisherman. Before Jesus called him to discipleship, John was assisting in the family fishing business.

John was one of the "inner circle" of three apostles who were permitted to be present with Jesus on very special occasions. In the early days of the church John teamed up with Peter. In his old age John was exiled to the island of Patmos. He was the last apostle to die.

The Gospel of John contains twenty-one chapters, 879 verses, and 19,099 words.

Situation

The date usually assigned to the Gospel of John is AD 90. Recently some, however, are suggesting that John's writings should be dated before the fall of Jerusalem to the Romans in AD 70.

Just before the destruction of Jerusalem (AD 70) John seems to have gone to the city of Ephesus on the western coast of modern

Turkey. He was eventually exiled by the Romans for a time to the island of Patmos.

According to tradition John wrote this Gospel in Ephesus. Whereas Matthew wrote for a Jewish audience, Mark for Romans, and Luke for Greeks, John's intended audience was everyone.

Plan

The Gospel of John includes such literary forms as narrative, parable, discourse, and dialog. John is the most selective, topical, and theological of the Gospels. The fourth Gospel was written over twenty years after the Gospel of Mark.

Structural plan. John organizes his material in five divisions:

- ❖ **Incarnation of the Son** (1:1-18)
- ❖ **Presentation of the Son** (1:19-4:54)
- ❖ **Opposition to the Son** (5:1-12:50)
- ❖ **Preparation by the Son** (13:1-17:26)
- ❖ **Vindication of the Son** (18:1-21:25)

Biographical plan. Like the other Gospels, John focuses on Jesus. He makes clear that Jesus was the eternal Word of God who became flesh and dwelled among us. The Twelve Apostles are also prominent, as in the previous Gospels. Others who are prominent are Nicodemus (*nih-kuh-dee'-muhs*), the Jewish leader who came to Jesus for teaching by night; and Pilate, the Roman governor who permitted the crucifixion of Jesus.

Geographical plan. John's Gospel makes a unique contribution to our knowledge of the life of Christ in the geographical area. John covers the same terrain as his predecessors; but he also reports on an early Judean ministry that is not referenced in Matthew, Mark, or Luke.

Chronological plan. John makes clear that Jesus attended at least four Jewish feasts in Jerusalem during his ministry. This information enables scholars to establish a rather exact chronological outline of the life of our Master.

Eternal Purpose

The immediate purpose of the Gospel of John is set forth by the writer himself: *these are written that you might believe that Jesus is the Christ, the Son of God, and that by believing you may have life in his name* (20:31). The ultimate purpose of the book is to provide information not included in the earlier Gospels, and to establish the deity of Christ.

In this Gospel the response to the claims of Jesus is the ultimate watershed of life. Those who believe that Jesus is the Son of God possess eternal life, but those who reject his claims live under the condemnation of God. In the first chapter of this Gospel, John introduces this theme: *He came to that which was his own, but his own did not receive him. Yet to all who received him, to those who believed in his name, he gave the right to become children of God* (1:11-12). Over and over in chapters 2–19 John documents the sad fact that most of Jesus' own people rejected him. There was, however, a remnant who committed their lives to the Lord.

John's Gospel contains several lengthy discourses of Jesus. John uses the discourses to explain the true significance of the "signs" that are identified in the narratives. Questions and objections help to develop the theme of each discourse. Jesus hammered home his main points by saying the same thing over and over again in different ways.

Acclaim

John paints his portrait of Jesus as **Son of God**. He presents the most powerful case in the Bible for the deity of Christ. This truth is underscored by John in four ways. First, John emphasizes the preexistence of Christ (ch. 1). Our Lord was present at creation. In fact, he was instrumental in creation. Second, John sets forth seven signs of Christ's deity (chs. 1–12). These include turning water to wine (ch. 2), walking on the water (6:19), and the resurrection of Lazarus (ch. 12). Third, Jesus made seven great claims in this Gospel. These are known as the "I am" claims. Among these are the following: *I am the way and the truth and the life* (14:6); *I am the light of the world* (9:5); *I am the vine; you are the branches* (15:5). Fourth, Jesus set forth five witnesses to his identity (5:30-40).

Keys

The key chapter in the Gospel of John is chapter 3. This chapter contains the testimony of John the Baptist. It also relates the conversation with Nicodemus that clearly points out that being born again is essential to enter the kingdom of heaven.

The key verse in the book is this: *These [signs] are written that you may believe that Jesus is the Christ, the Son of God* (20:31).

The key phrase in the book is *I am* (93).

Key words in the fourth Gospel are *truth* (57), *believe/faith* (57), *love* (27), *light* (24), and *word* (22).

Special Features

Here are some facts that render the Gospel of John special in the sacred collection:

- ❖ John's Gospel has the clearest purpose statement in the Bible.
- ❖ The expression *doubting Thomas*, which describes a skeptic, is based on the portrayal of the Apostle Thomas in John's Gospel.
- ❖ In Christian art the symbol for the Gospel of John was a soaring eagle.
- ❖ John's Gospel is the most theological of the four Gospels.
- ❖ In John's Gospel *the Jews* is a technical term that refers to the opponents of Jesus, not all people who are racially Jews.

HEAR

Here are some of the outstanding chapters in the fourth Gospel:

- ❖ John's introduction to Jesus (John 1)
- ❖ Jesus' first miracle (John 2)
- ❖ Resurrection of Lazarus (John 11–12)
- ❖ Jesus' washing of the disciples' feet (John 13)
- ❖ Jesus' Upper Room discourse (John 14–16)
- ❖ Jesus' high priestly prayer (John 17)

Here are some of the favorite verses in John's Gospel:
- ❖ *I was blind but now I see* (9:25).
- ❖ *For God so loved the world, that he gave his one and only Son, that whoever believes in him shall not perish but have eternal life* (3:16).
- ❖ *I am the bread of life* (6:35).
- ❖ *Do not let your hearts be troubled* (14:1).
- ❖ *I will ask the Father, and he will give you another Counselor* (14:16).

Summary of the Foundation Books			
Book	**Audience**	**Jesus View**	**Emphasis**
Matthew	Jews	Sovereign	Fulfilled prophecy
Mark	Romans	Servant	How he worked
Luke	Greeks	Son of Man	What he was like
John	Everyone	Son of God	Who he really was

Section Two

FRAMEWORK BOOK

Acts of the Apostles

Chapter Four

LUKE'S SECOND VOLUME
Acts of the Apostles

Acts functions in the New Testament like the twelve historical books function in the Old Testament library. Acts relates the history of about the first three decades of the church. Many of the epistles that follow in the New Testament fit into the historical framework provided by Acts.

44th Book of the Bible
Acts of the Apostles
Proclamation of the Gospel

The fifth book of the New Testament was known in the ancient church by the name *Acts of the Apostles* or simply *Acts*. The name in some respects is a misnomer. Acts only relates the details of the ministry of two of the apostles, Peter and Paul. Because of Luke's strong emphasis on the ministry of the Holy Spirit, some have suggested that this book should really be called the *Acts of the Holy Spirit*.

The opening verses of Acts make the point that this book is the second book in a two-volume set. Both Luke and Acts are addressed to Theophilus. He was a wealthy Christian patron who probably financed the production of this monumental set. Luke identifies the occasions when he was personally present by using the plural "we" or "us."

The Book of Acts contains twenty-eight chapters, 1,007 verses, and 24,250 words.

Situation

Acts concludes by relating how Paul was in custody in Rome for two years. A date of about AD 63 for the writing can be assigned.

During his travels with Paul Luke met many of the Christian leaders. He was in a position to gather the facts about the earliest days of the church. On some of Paul's missionary trips, Luke personally was present. Because he was interested in preserving the history of the church, and because he as much as any other was in a position to know the facts about Christianity, Luke penned the Book of Acts.

Plan

The Book of Acts consists largely of lively narrative punctuated here and there with prayers and sermons. The theme of the book is *witnessing for Christ.*

Structural plan. Acts unfolds geographically as outlined in Acts 1:8. Thus an outline of the book looks like this:

- **Introduction** (ch. 1)
- **Jerusalem Campaign** (2:1–8:3)
- **Judea–Samaria Campaign** (8:4–12:25)
- **Worldwide Campaign** (chs. 13–28)

The writer of Acts was a missionary himself. He personally participated in much of the history that he narrates in this book. His account, therefore, is not the detached analysis of an historian reviewing the past. Luke writes with passion about missions, for missions were his life. This in no way, however, detracts from the authority of this primary historical document. Luke can properly be designated the first church historian.

Geographical plan. Acts needs to be studied with a Bible atlas in hand. There are about eighty geographical references in Acts.

Four major **regions** are mentioned. First, **Judea** is the region around Jerusalem. In the first century this region was administered by a Roman governor who was headquartered in the seacoast city of Caesarea. Second, the region of **Samaria** was north of Judea. During his ministry Jesus had sowed the seed in that region. Philip the preaching deacon was the first Christian to carry the gospel into Samaria. Third, **Asia Minor** was the ancient name for the country we now call Turkey. In New Testament times that region was carved up into fourteen Roman provinces, all of which are mentioned in Acts. The fourth major area of activity in Acts is **Greece**. In this period the northern half of Greece was called Macedonia, the southern half Achaia. Paul spent a great deal of time in the region of Greece.

In addition to the four major areas, five major **cities** are the centers for the activity in Acts: Jerusalem, Antioch, Corinth, Ephesus, and Rome. The church was founded in **Jerusalem**. There the Christians remained for four or five years until forced to scatter by persecution. Jerusalem remained a strong center of the faith until the Romans destroyed the city in AD 70.

Persecution caused the Christians to carry the message as far as **Antioch**, three hundred miles north of Jerusalem. Barnabas teamed up with Saul (later called Paul) to teach the new Gentile believers in that city. Antioch was the hub of missionary endeavor for many years.

Paul founded the church in **Corinth** on his second missionary journey. Paul wrote two letters to the church in Corinth. Several of the greatest New Testament preachers spent time ministering in Corinth.

Paul used **Ephesus** on the western coast of modern Turkey as a hub for evangelizing the Roman province called Asia. After the fall of Jerusalem in AD 70 Ephesus seems to have become the main center of Christianity. The Apostle John spent his last years there.

Rome was the center of the Roman world. We do not know how the church came to be founded there. It already existed when Paul wrote his letter to the Romans. Paul was in custody in Rome on two occasions. He, along with Peter, was martyred there about the year AD 68.

Biographical structure. In the three evangelistic campaigns referenced in the outline above, **Peter and John** are the leaders in the first, **Peter and Philip** in the second, and **Paul** in the third. Luke mentions over one hundred people by name in Acts. Aside from the campaign leaders, the key figures in this book are **Stephen,** a preaching deacon; three notable converts **Simon the Sorcerer,** the Roman centurion **Cornelius** *(kor-nee'-lee-us),* and **Lydia,** the first European convert to Christianity; four great missionaries: **Barnabas** *(bahr'-nuh-buhs),* **Silas** *(si'-luhs),* **Timothy,** and **Luke**; and **James,** the half brother of Jesus who became a leader in the Jerusalem church.

Chronological structure. The Book of Acts reports the history of the earliest Christians from the *enthronement* of Jesus (AD 30) to the Roman *imprisonment* of Paul (AD 63). Therefore, Acts covers roughly thirty-four years.

Eternal Purpose

The immediate purpose of the Book of Acts is to continue the record of what Jesus began to do and to teach (1:1). The ultimate purpose of this book is to document that the power of God and the guidance of the Holy Spirit were present in the formative days of the Christian church.

Acts is valuable for showing how the early Christians evangelized—how they presented the gospel plan of salvation. Luke has selected a number of conversion cases to illustrate how one by one the barriers to the spread of the gospel were smashed. A large crowd on the Jewish feast day of Pentecost contained at least some who had been responsible for the crucifixion of Jesus. Peter's message convicted them of this terrible sin and drove them to ask how they might obtain God's forgiveness. The response, *repent and be baptized* (Acts 2:38), is the first presentation of the gospel plan during the reign of Christ.

One of the great benefits of Acts is the way it illustrates how the Christians responded to Christ's Great Commission to carry the gospel to the ends of the earth (Matthew 28:19f). It took the Christians about ten years to catch up to the spirit of Christ's commission. A persecution got the Christians out of Jerusalem. Philip the preaching deacon took that occasion to break through the Samaritan barrier. A few years later a housetop vision convinced Peter to preach the gospel to Gentiles for the first time. Even after this breakthrough many Jewish Christians resisted the full inclusion of Gentiles in the life of the church. Ultimately the view of Paul prevailed. The gospel was carried to the far corners of the Roman Empire.

In Acts Luke traces the history of that crucial generation when the makeup of the church shifted from predominantly Jewish membership to predominantly Gentile membership. Luke intends to demonstrate that the church is not one of many branches of Judaism. In Acts he presents the church as the new and true Israel of God—as the ultimate fulfillment of Old Testament aspiration and anticipation. In the church the true sons of Abraham are manifested, the destiny of ancient Israel is fulfilled.

Another valuable contribution of Acts is the background material it furnishes for the interpretation of the Epistles of Paul. Without Acts many of the allusions in Paul's letters would be difficult if not impossible to understand.

Acclaim

In Acts Jesus is portrayed as the **Enthroned King.** New Testament preachers cited Old Testament prophecy to prove that the resurrection/ascension of Christ was anticipated and thus required. The apostles throughout the book bear testimony to having seen Christ alive after his crucifixion. They had forty days to establish the reality of his astonishing conquest of death.

In Acts 1 eleven apostles saw Christ ascend into heaven (Acts 1:9). Peter offered tangible proof that Jesus was enthroned in heaven by pointing to the outpouring of the Holy Spirit with accompanying signs that transpired on the day of Pentecost (Acts

2:32-35). Just before his martyr's death Stephen claimed to have seen the heavens opened. He saw the glory of God and Jesus standing at the right hand of God (Acts 7:56). On the Damascus road Saul of Tarsus saw a blinding light from heaven and heard the voice of Jesus (Acts 9:3-6). This same event is told in the words of Paul himself in 22:6-10 and 26:13-18. Clearly the Christians made the heavenly enthronement of Jesus one of the key points in their message (Acts 17:7).

Keys

The key chapter in the Book of Acts is chapter 10. This chapter records the conversion of the first Gentile.

The key verse in the book is this: *you [apostles] will receive power when the Holy Spirit comes on you; and you will be my witnesses in Jerusalem, and in all Judea and Samaria, and to the ends of the earth* (Acts 1:8). As noted above, this verse virtually outlines the contents of the book.

The key phrases in the book are *and it came to pass* (13 KJV) and *passed through* (8).

Key words include *believe/believed/faith* (55) and *baptized/baptism* (27).

Special Features

Here are some interesting facts about Acts that set this book apart in the books of Scripture:

- ❖ The earliest name for believers in Christ was *followers of the Way*. The term *Christian* did not surface until about a decade after Christ.
- ❖ The two books of Luke and Acts make up twenty-eight percent of the New Testament.
- ❖ Acts contains the last recorded words of Jesus (Acts 1:8).
- ❖ Acts is the historical link between the Gospels and the Epistles. It provides historical background for ten of Paul's letters.
- ❖ Luke's precision in citing locations and titles (e.g., consul, tetrarch) has been verified by archaeological evidence.

❖ Acts devotes a large amount of space to speeches and sermons. There are no less than twenty-four messages in the twenty-eight chapters of the book.

HEAR

God speaks his will for the church in the Book of Acts. The church needs to hear what the Lord says. Here are some of the outstanding chapters in Acts that can serve as a start for your detailed study of the book:

❖ Final days of Jesus (Acts 1)
❖ Birthday of the church (Acts 2)
❖ Conversion of Saul of Tarsus (Acts 9)
❖ Conversion of the first Gentile (Acts 10)
❖ Paul's 1st missionary journey (Acts 13–14)
❖ The Jerusalem council (Acts 15)
❖ Paul's 2nd missionary journey (Acts 16–18)
❖ Paul's voyage to Rome (Acts 21)

Here are some favorite lines from Acts:

❖ *Everyone who calls on the name of the Lord will be saved* (2:21).
❖ *Repent and be baptized, every one of you* (2:38).
❖ *We must obey God rather than men* (5:29).
❖ *God is no respecter of persons* (10:34 KJV).
❖ *Believe in the Lord Jesus, and you will be saved* (16:31).
❖ *It is more blessed to give than to receive* (Acts 20:35).
❖ *And now, what are you waiting for? Get up, be baptized and wash your sins away* (22:16).
❖ *Almost you persuade me to be a Christian* (26:28 KJV).

Section Three

FAITH BOOKS

Romans
1 Corinthians
2 Corinthians
Galatians
Ephesians
Philippians
Colossians
1 Thessalonians
2 Thessalonians
1 Timothy
2 Timothy
Titus
Philemon

Chapter Five

EVANGELICAL EPISTLES
Romans & Galatians

Thus far we have completed two of the shelves in the New Testament library—the foundation books and the framework book. With this lesson we begin our survey of the faith books—essentially the Pauline letters. These letters set forth the details of the Christian faith.

The letter to the Galatians is here treated out of order with Romans for two reasons. First, both letters were written from Corinth at about the same time. Second, both Romans and Galatians deal with the same subject matter. In fact, some have referred to Galatians as the outline for the more extended treatment of Romans. Others have likened Galatians to a rough sketch of which Romans is the finished picture. Nineteen passages in the two epistles are similar.

Romans and Galatians together are Paul's *evangelical epistles* because of their emphasis on salvation by faith. The theme of these epistles is **Christ and the Cross**. Paul teaches us in Romans and Galatians to look back to the Cross if we would have our faith strengthened. The practical side of the evangelical epistles is that we (Christians) have been raised with Christ from deadness and barrenness to life and fruitfulness.

45th Book of the Bible
Book of Romans
Facts of Our Faith

The author of Romans is Paul. This is the first of thirteen of his epistles.

Paul grew up in the city of Tarsus in the province of Cilicia, part of modern-day Turkey. He studied in Jerusalem under the great rabbi Gamaliel (Acts 22:3). He was in Jerusalem when Stephen was stoned as the first Christian martyr. The killers laid their outer garments at the feet of Paul (then called Saul) during the execution. Paul led out in the first serious persecution of the Christians. While on the road to Damascus to arrest Christians, Christ confronted this persecutor. As a result Saul of Tarsus became a believer.

Immediately Paul began to preach in the synagogues in Damascus. The Lord then led Paul into the Arabian Desert for some private instruction in Christian teaching. Later Paul went to Jerusalem where he met Peter and James and other leaders in the church. When the Jerusalem Jews hatched a plot against him, Paul left Palestine and returned to Tarsus. There he remained until Barnabas came to invite him to join the teaching staff in the fast-growing congregation at Antioch. Following a trip to Jerusalem carrying money for the poor saints there, the church at Antioch sent forth Barnabas and Paul on an extended missionary journey.

The Book of Romans contains sixteen chapters, 433 verses, and 9,447 words. Partly because of its length Romans was placed at the beginning of the Pauline letters in our Bible. Even more important in this placement is the fact that Romans provides the doctrinal foundation upon which the apostle's other epistles are built.

Situation

Scholars assign a date of about AD 56 to Romans. That means that the letter was written about twenty-six years after the founding of the church.

On his Third Missionary Journey Paul traveled from Ephesus to Greece (Corinth) where he remained for three months (Acts 20:2-3). While there, Paul wrote his two evangelical epistles, Romans and Galatians. The writing was triggered by the realization that he would not be able to visit Rome any time soon (Romans 15:22-29; 16:1, 23).

Plan

Romans follows the regular form of letters in Paul's day. Interspersed here and there in the epistle are doxologies or praise sections. In a style reminiscent of Malachi, Paul in places uses a very effective question-and-answer format to make the most systematic presentation of Christian doctrine (teaching) in the Bible. The questions that Paul raises and answers probably reflect the kinds of objections to the gospel that he had encountered during two decades of missionary travels. Romans is the most formal of Paul's writings. It often reads more like a treatise than a letter.

Structural plan. Romans focuses on the theme *the Facts of Our Faith*. Following an introduction Romans is organized into three main divisions. The main body of the epistle is followed by a lengthy conclusion. The outline for Romans looks like this:

- ❖ **Introduction** (1:1-17)
- ❖ **God's Righteousness Revealed** (1:18-8:39)
- ❖ **God's Righteousness Vindicated** (9:1-11:36)
- ❖ **God's Righteousness Applied** (12:1-15:13)
- ❖ **Conclusion** (15:14-16:27)

In the first main division Paul speaks on the themes of the condemnation of all men because of sin, the justification of believers through faith, and the sanctification or setting apart of Christians from the world. Justification means that God treats those who have turned to Christ just as if they have never sinned. In the second main division Paul speaks about Israel past, present, and future. In the third main division Paul shows how the principles of the faith apply both in duties and liberties.

Another even more concise outline for Romans is this: doctrinal section (1:1–8:39), national section (9:1–11:36) and practical section (12:1–16:27).

Biographical plan. Besides Paul the writer, Romans mentions a host of the apostle's fellow workers—at least twenty-seven (Romans 16:1-15). In this list there are Greek names and Jewish names; there are women and men; there are simple folk and city officials, and no doubt poor and rich. This list of Christian workers illustrates the unity that Paul advocated for Christian congregations.

Geographical plan. The point of origin for this letter was Corinth in Achaia (southern Greece). The destination of the letter was Rome, capital of the Empire. In Paul's day the city had a population well over a million. One inscription puts its population at four million. The great success of the Roman armies abroad brought wealth to the city. Rome was known for its architecture, games, and modern conveniences.

The Roman population included a great many imported slaves. Consequently the city was religiously diverse. Accompanying the foreign population were not only their religions, but also their vices. Rome was a city known for its sin. Regular programs of combat until death were conducted in the arenas. The "games" might include mock warfare, hand-to-hand combat between trained fighters known as gladiators, or combat with exotic beasts imported from distant lands.

Little is known concerning the origin of the Roman church. Romans indicates that the congregation was primarily composed of Gentile Christians. One can conclude from reading Romans that the church was doctrinally sound. Paul devotes no space to refuting errors in this congregation. In fact he commends these Christians (1:8). Paul's desire to come to them that he might communicate to them some spiritual gift (1:11) suggests that no apostles had yet visited the city of Rome.

In this letter Paul anticipates a trip to Spain (15:24, 28). Early Christian literature testifies that Paul eventually was able to carry out this intention.

Eternal Purpose

The immediate purpose of the Epistle to the Romans is to prepare the brethren in Rome for Paul's long-awaited visit and to build up these believers in their knowledge, faith, and fellowship. This epistle is more preventative than corrective. On a more practical level, Paul may have been trying to gain financial, moral, and prayer support for two upcoming projects: 1) a preaching mission to Spain (15:24), and 2) a collection for the poor in Jerusalem (15:30-31). The ultimate purpose of the book is to explain that the gift of God's righteousness comes to everyone by faith in Christ.

A synopsis of Romans looks like this: We are saved by faith, not by the Mosaic Law or good works. The saved have died to the old life. They must live righteously. All who are saved, Jew or Gentile, are part of the new Israel of God. The redeemed community has civic and social responsibilities.

Romans focuses on relationships between Jews and Gentiles. This may hint that tensions between the two groups existed in this church. Paul argues that neither group can feel superior to the other. Both alike require a righteousness that can be obtained only as a gift of God. This God-given righteousness must be lived out in the personal and congregational life of the Christian. For Paul Christianity was a lifestyle motivated by a belief system revealed by God. The gospel is more than a set of facts to be acknowledged; it is a life to be lived.

Acclaim

In Romans Paul paints a portrait of Jesus primarily as the **Redeemer** (1:17). Christ is the Second Adam whose righteous life and atoning death have provided justification for all who place their faith in him. Romans explores the significance of Christ's death as a sacrifice for mankind's sin. His death and resurrection are the basis for the believer's forgiveness of sin, reconciliation with God, salvation from judgment wrath and glorification in the world to come.

Keys

The key chapters in Romans are chapters 6–8. These chapters contain instructions on how to live a balanced life under grace through the power of the Holy Spirit.

Without question the key verse is this: *I am not ashamed of the gospel, because it is the power of God for the salvation of everyone who believes: first for the Jew, then for the Gentile* (Romans 1:16).

The key phrase in the book is *by faith* (8).

Key words include *righteous/righteousness* (43), *faith/believe/believed* (57), *law* (78), and *sin/sinned* (51).

Special Features

Some facts and opinions about Romans make this epistle stand out in the collection of New Testament books.

- ❖ Romans is one of the most forceful, logical, and eloquent works ever penned. It probably has influenced the subsequent history of the church more than any other epistle.
- ❖ While the Gospels present the facts of Christ's life, Romans expounds the significance of those facts.
- ❖ The uncharacteristically long introduction to this epistle (1:1-16) probably is to be explained by the fact that Paul is writing to a church he had never visited.
- ❖ Unlike his other letters, Paul uses no title for himself in Romans (other than *servant*).
- ❖ Romans abounds in Old Testament quotations.
- ❖ Archaeologists found a block of pavement stone in Corinth bearing the name of Erastus, commissioner of public works. This may be the same Corinthian Christian and city treasurer that Paul mentioned in Romans 16:23.
- ❖ The conclusion of Romans is unique in that Paul addresses a comparatively large group of individuals.

HEAR

Romans is not easy reading. The early chapters may make some think they are reading a syllabus for an advanced theology class. You need to wade through this theology. Try to grasp each step in Paul's argument. These chapters are important because they explain why Christians believe and behave the way they do. The letter winds down, however, with a few chapters of easy-reading, practical advice about everyday living.

Romans sets forth the message of God in a profound way. This book requires us to listen carefully and thoughtfully. Here are some of the outstanding chapters in Romans with which you can sample the contents of this book:

- Corruption of the human race (Romans 1)
- Dead to sin, alive to God (Romans 6)
- Salvation from sin and suffering (Romans 8)
- Gentiles grafted into the Israel tree (Romans 11)
- The transformed life (Romans 12)

Here are a few of the famous lines in the Book of Romans:

- *The wages of sin is death, but the gift of God is eternal life in Christ Jesus our Lord* (6:23).
- *All have sinned and fall short of the glory of God* (3:23).
- *We know that in all things God works for the good of those who love him, who have been called according to his purpose* (8:28).
- *Who shall separate us from the love of Christ?* (8:35).
- *We were therefore buried with him through baptism into death* (6:4).
- *If you confess with your mouth, "Jesus is Lord," and believe in your heart that God raised him from the dead, you will be saved* (10:9).

48th Book of the Bible
Book of Galatians
Freedom of Our Faith

The reasons for pairing Romans and Galatians in this survey were noted at the beginning of this chapter. In many ways Galatians is a synopsis of Romans. While the two letters are similar in many respects, there is a different tone in Galatians. Romans deals with the issues systematically. In Galatians Paul treats the same issues argumentatively. Paul is a teacher in Romans, a debater in Galatians. The harsh words of Galatians are the language of conflict. The apostle was shocked at the digression from the gospel that had taken place among his converts in such a short period of time. Paul's emotionally charged language reflects the urgency of the situation.

Galatians contains six chapters, 149 verses, and 3,098 words.

Situation

Prior to writing his letter to the Galatians, Paul had traveled in the region of Galatia (in the area of modern Turkey) three times. In fact, Paul was the founding minister of many of the churches in that region. Scholars think that Galatians was written from the city of Corinth on Paul's third missionary journey. This epistle was probably written at the same time as Romans, about AD 56.

The writing of this letter was triggered by news of Judaizers subverting the gospel of God's grace among the Galatian churches. Some Judaizers insisted that one had to become a Jew before he could become a Christian. Others conceded that one could be a Christian without obedience to the Law, but only a second class Christian.

Plan

In the epistle to the Galatians Paul shows great versatility in his presentation by utilizing Scripture, experience, logic, warning, and exhortation to make his points.

Structural plan. The letter breaks down into three main divisions with an introduction and conclusion as "bookends" at beginning and end. The theme of this letter is the *Freedom of our Faith*. The great doctrine that is set forth in this book is that of salvation by God's grace through faith in Christ. The outline looks like this:

- ❖ **Introduction** (1:1-10)
- ❖ **Derivation of the Doctrine** (1:11–2:21)
- ❖ **Vindication of the Doctrine** (chs. 3–4)
- ❖ **Application of the Doctrine** (5:1–6:10)
- ❖ **Conclusion** (6:11-18)

In the first main division, Paul defends his authority as an apostle of Jesus Christ. In the second, Paul defends the principle of salvation by faith. In the third division, Paul draws out the implications of this great doctrine.

Biographical plan. Galatians focuses on Paul himself. Here Paul fills in the gaps in our knowledge about his earliest years as a Christian. In this letter the apostle comes across as a man of great courage, tenderness, earnestness, sincerity, and burning devotion to Christ.

Paul mentions two of his associates in Galatians. **Titus** (*ti'-tuhs*) was a Gentile convert whom Paul refused to circumcise as the Judaizers demanded. Paul took Titus with him to the Jerusalem conference of church leaders as a "test case" regarding the necessity of circumcision. **Barnabas,** Paul's companion on the first missionary journey, also accompanied Paul to the Jerusalem conference in AD 51.

Galatians alludes to three of the prominent leaders of the church in Jerusalem. **James** the Lord's half brother, **Cephas/Peter** and the Apostle **John.** Paul says of these three that they *were reported to be pillars* in the church.

Galatians also mentions four prominent Old Testament characters: **Abraham, Isaac** (*i'-zahk*), **Hagar** (*hay'-gahr*), and by implication **Sarah**.

Geographical plan. As the name of the letter implies, the focus of this epistle is on the province of Galatia. This was a strip of territory roughly three hundred miles long and a hundred miles wide, located in what is today western Turkey. After Galatia was made a Roman province in 25 BC, various rulers added and deleted territory. So the boundaries of Galatia were somewhat fluid. Scholars debate whether Paul intended the letter for churches he founded in southern Galatia on his first missionary journey (churches named in Scripture), or churches he started in northern Galatia on his second missionary journey (not named in Scripture).

In Galatians Paul alludes to several regions through which he passed in his travels. Besides Galatia itself, these regions include *Arabia; Syria; Cilicia* (*sih-lish'-ih-uh*), his home area in southern Turkey; and *Judea*.

In particular Paul mentions three cities that he had visited at the time of the writing of this letter: **Damascus, Jerusalem,** and **Antioch.** Galatians reports an interesting confrontation between Peter and Paul at Antioch (2:11-14).

One Old Testament location is named in the letter: **Mount Sinai** (4:24-25).

Eternal Purpose

The immediate purpose of the Epistle to the Galatians is to respond to reports that the Galatian churches were being subverted by false teaching. Judaizers were trying to bring Gentile Christians under the yoke of the Mosaic Law. The deeper purpose of the letter is to establish the principle that people are justified before God through faith in Christ apart from any works of the Law.

A synopsis of Galatians looks like this: Those who teach salvation by works have perverted the gospel. Paul vindicates the gospel of grace that he had been preaching (1:11–2:14). He stresses the superiority of his gospel to the Law of Moses. The basic truth brought out in this book is that Christians are free from the bondage of Mosaic Law. Because Christ paid the penalty for our sin on the cross, the believer has been delivered from the curse of sin, Law, and self.

Intertwined with the heavy theology of Galatians there is also a very practical and personal element. It is this letter that stresses the futility of our struggling in our own strength to do what is right. Here we learn the secret of victorious living. This involves allowing the Holy Spirit to renew us from within. It is God who enables us to engage in good and loving acts that demonstrate the reality of Christ enthroned in our hearts. The gospel offers not only salvation from our sin, but victory over self as well.

Acclaim

Galatians suggests that Christ is not only our Savior, he is our **Liberator.** As Christians we have been liberated from the bondage of the Law—what some call legalism. Legalism is the attempt to dot every "i" and cross every "t" of divine commands so as to make ourselves worthy of heaven. Legalism leads to misery and uncertainty. One can never be sure that he has done enough to require God to save him.

Christ has also liberated the believer from the bondage to sin or license. A life without boundaries is a life in chaos. Sin corrupts, drags down and ultimately destroys. Christ living within us gives us direction, purpose, and liberty—freedom to live happy, useful, and productive lives apart from sin.

Keys

The key chapter in the Epistle to the Galatians is chapter 5. In this chapter Paul forcefully makes the point that liberty is not license to do as we please.

The key verse in the book is this: *No one is justified before God by the law* (Galatians 3:11).

The key phrase in the book is *Jesus Christ/Christ Jesus* (16).

Key words include first person pronouns (121), *but* (51), *law* (34), *faith* (22), *if* (21), *spirit* (18), and *flesh* (18).

Special Features

A number of things distinguish Galatians within the collection of New Testament books:

- ❖ This is the most emotionally charged book of the Bible. One can sense Paul's disappointment, even disgust, as he "unloads" on the wayward Galatians.

- Many scholars regard Galatians as the earliest of Paul's letters — dating from just after his first missionary journey in AD 49. (A better case can be made for 1 Thessalonians as Paul's earliest letter.)
- Galatians is the only epistle Paul addressed to a group of churches.
- Galatians may have been the only book written personally by the apostle without the aid of a stenographer (6:11).
- Compared with Paul's other letters, there are notable omissions in Galatians: no word of commendation, praise, or thanksgiving; no request for prayer; no mention of the present activity of his companions; no mention of the Galatians' standing in Christ.
- Martin Luther so loved this book that he called it by his wife's name. He said, "I am wedded to it." For this reason Galatians was the masthead of the Reformation.

HEAR

God speaks clearly on the subject of Christian liberty in the Epistle to the Galatians. We need to hear what this book says. Here are a couple outstanding chapters where you can "get your feet wet" in the study of this book.

- Sons of Abraham and sons of God (Galatians 3).
- Our duty to fellow believers (Galatians 6).

Some of the favorite lines from the Epistle to the Galatians are these:

- *Do not be deceived: God cannot be mocked. A man reaps what he sows* (Galatians 6:7).
- *I have been crucified with Christ and I no longer live, but Christ lives in me* (2:20).
- *You are all sons of God through faith in Christ Jesus, for all of you who were baptized into Christ have clothed yourselves with Christ* (3:26-27).

❖ *May I never boast except in the cross of our Lord Jesus Christ . . . (6:14).*
❖ *But the fruit of the Spirit is love, joy, peace, patience, kindness, goodness, faithfulness, gentleness and self-control. Against such things there is no law. (5:22-23).*

Chapter Six

ENCOUNTER EPISTLES
1 & 2 Corinthians

Paul wrote two letters to the church in Corinth (Greece). The two letters were written about three months apart. We may designate these companion letters as Paul's *encounter epistles*. In them he confronts head on the issues in the church and the attacks on his apostleship. One might list as the theme of the two Corinthian letters **Christ and the Critics**. If faith looked back to the cross in the two evangelical epistles, in the encounter epistles faith looks down to the foundation and is measured.

46th Book of the Bible
Book of 1 Corinthians
Discipline of the Church

The writer of 1 Corinthians is Paul. He founded the church at Corinth on his second missionary journey. There he met two fellow tentmakers, Aquila and Priscilla, and led them to Christ. During his eighteen months in the city Paul baptized the ruler of the synagogue. He was hauled into court by antagonistic Jews; but the case was thrown out by the proconsul Gallio.

The first epistle to the Corinthians contains sixteen chapters, 437 verses, and 9,489 words.

Situation

A date of about AD 55 can be assigned to 1 Corinthians. This is about three years following Paul's initial visit to the city. While in Ephesus, Paul wrote a letter to Corinth that has not survived (1 Corinthians 5:9). He sent Timothy and Erastus into Achaia (southern Greece) to check on the Corinth work (Acts 19:21f). Having received reports from Chloe's people and some specific questions, Paul wrote 1 Corinthians (1 Corinthians 1:11). He told the Corinthians to expect a visit from Timothy soon. Paul himself anticipated coming to Corinth shortly to deal with the problems there. For the moment, however, obligations in Ephesus did not permit him to come.

Plan

Obviously 1 Corinthians has the epistolary format, i.e., it is written in the style of a letter of that day. Paul used nearly every literary device known to writing in this letter including logic, sarcasm, entreaty, scolding, poetry, narration, and exposition.

Structural plan. The first Corinthian epistle has two major sections with an introduction and a conclusion. The theme of the book is the ***discipline of faith***. The outline looks like this:

- ❖ **Introduction** (1:1-9)
- ❖ **Seven Corruptions** (1:10–6:20)
- ❖ **Six Questions** (7:1–16:12)
- ❖ **Conclusion** (16:13-24)

In the first major section Paul prescribes correction for various problems in the church at Corinth. In the second major section he presents instruction in respect to various questions that had been submitted to him.

Biographical plan. Obviously the person about whom the most is said in 1 Corinthians is the writer, Paul himself. As the founder of the church Paul regarded himself as the spiritual father of the Corinthians.

This epistle alludes to two Old Testament characters (**Adam; Moses**) and fourteen Christian leaders and associates. The most important of these are **Cephas** (*see'-fuhs*) or Simon Peter, who is mentioned four times, and **Apollos** (*ay-pahl'-lahs*), who is mentioned seven times.

Apollos was a disciple of John the Baptist when he encountered Priscilla and Aquila in Ephesus. They taught this man the word of the Lord more perfectly (Acts 18:26). Apollos became a powerful preacher of the gospel. He went from Ephesus to Greece with the encouragement of the Asian believers and a letter of introduction (Acts 18:27). Apollos greatly strengthened the believers in Corinth by using the Scriptures to demonstrate that Jesus was the Christ (Acts 18:28). Apollos is last mentioned in the Book of Acts as being in Corinth (19:1). There he became a popular preacher, considered by some the equal of Peter and Paul.

In 1 Corinthians 16:12 Apollos is called *our brother*, indicating that Paul considered him as one of the team. Paul asked Titus to help Apollos on his way (Titus 3:13). Because of Apollos's knowledge of the Old Testament, Luther suggested that Apollos might be the writer of the Book of Hebrews.

Geographical plan. The city of Corinth was strategically located on the piece of land connecting ancient Macedonia (northern Greece) with Achaia. Corinth had two seaports, Cenchrea on the side of the Aegean Sea and Lechaeum on the edge of the Gulf of Corinth. The city was a thriving trade center due to its location. It was a port of call for merchant and military vessels. Corinth became world renowned for its wickedness. The term *Corinthian* meant a profligate; to *Corinthianize* meant to engage in the most repulsive sexual immorality.

The first letter to the Corinthians was written from Ephesus in the province of Asia. See description of Ephesus under Ephesians.

Eternal Purpose

The immediate purpose of 1 Corinthians is to address certain questions from Corinth and certain abuses in the church there. The deeper purpose of the epistle is to stress the truths that the church must be disciplined in practice and pure in doctrine.

In synopsis 1 Corinthians addresses such questions as disunity, fornication, litigation, mixed marriages, unmarried virgins, food sacrificed to idols, and abuse of spiritual gifts. It stresses the importance of love (ch. 13) and the doctrine of the resurrection of Jesus (ch. 15). A basic truth taught in this book is this: we are set apart for the Lord by his Spirit.

An incidental contribution of 1 Corinthians is the insight it gives into the life of a Christian congregation in the days of the apostles. Much of what we know about a Christian assembly in the first century comes from this book.

Corinth was Paul's problem church. It bristled with social, ethical, spiritual, and doctrinal problems. The epistle is timely because, unfortunately, there's a little bit of Corinth in every church — a lot of Corinth in some. What congregation today does not deal from time to time with sexual and marriage issues, worship issues, division, discrimination, abuse of the Lord's Supper and spiritual gifts?

This epistle is gripping because of the deeply emotional issues Paul tackles. Yet his profound wisdom and insight dominate every page. Perhaps more than any other epistle, 1 Corinthians reveals Paul's patient love and self-control when confronted with outlandish behavior by fledging Christians.

The first letter to the Corinthians makes several important contributions to Christian teaching. Particularly valuable is its teaching about the nature of the church, the role of spiritual gifts, and the resurrection. Paul's appeal for unity within the body of Christ (the church) is one of the strongest in the New Testament. This epistle was designed to refute worldly attitudes and conduct that lead to division among believers.

Acclaim

In 1 Corinthians Paul refers to *Jesus* (1), *Lord Jesus* (3), *Christ* (36), *Jesus Christ* (7), and *Lord Jesus Christ* (10). The emphasis on the church as the body of Christ and his temple suggests that Paul stresses Christ as the **Sanctifier** *[of the Body]*. Christ not only saves us from the consequences of sin, he sets us apart from this sinful world as a special people.

1 & 2 Corinthians

Keys

The key chapter in 1 Corinthians is chapter 13. This chapter defines the nature of love as an action, not an emotion. It is without doubt the best known chapter in the epistle.

The key verse is this: *Don't you know that you yourselves are God's temple and that God's Spirit lives in you?* (3:16).

The key phrases include *our Lord Jesus Christ* (7) and *do you not know* (7).

Key words include *love* (17), *tongue/tongues* (22), *church* (18), and *wisdom* (18).

Special Features

Here are some distinguishing facts about 1 Corinthians:
- ❖ 1 Corinthians is Paul's longest epistle exceeding Romans by forty-two words.
- ❖ 1 Corinthians may not have been Paul's first letter to Corinth. In 1 Corinthians 5:9 he alludes to *my other letter*.
- ❖ While Paul was in Corinth in AD 51, the Isthmian Games were held in the city. This was an athletic competition held every four years. It was second in popularity only to the Olympics. These games probably formed the background for Paul's allusions to athletic metaphors in 1 Corinthians 9:24-25.

HEAR

Here are a few outstanding chapters from 1 Corinthians.
- ❖ Defense of Paul's apostleship (1 Corinthians 9)
- ❖ Great love chapter (1 Corinthians 13)
- ❖ Great resurrection chapter (1 Corinthians 15)

Some of the favorite verses in 1 Corinthians are these:
- ❖ *Where, O death, is your victory? Where, O death, is your sting?* (15:55).
- ❖ *No temptation has seized you except what is common to man. And God is faithful; he will not let you be tempted*

> beyond what you can bear. But when you are tempted, he will also provide a way out so that you can stand up under it. (10:13).

❖ Your body is a temple of the Holy Spirit (6:19).
❖ If I speak in the tongues of men and of angels, but have not love, I am am only a resounding gong, or a clanging cymbal (13:1).
❖ I appeal to you, brothers . . . that there may be no divisions among you (1:10).
❖ The message of the cross is foolishness to those who are perishing, but to us who are being saved it is the power of God (1:18).
❖ For no one can lay any foundation other than the one already laid, which is Jesus Christ (3:11).
❖ A man ought to examine himself before he eats of the bread and drinks of the cup (11:28).
❖ If Christ has not been raised, your faith is futile; you are still in your sins (15:17).

47th Book of the Bible
Book of 2 Corinthians
Defense of the Apostle

From ancient times the forty-seventh book of the Bible had the title *Pros Korinthious B = second to the Corinthians*. The writer of this epistle is Paul, the founder of the church at Corinth.

The second epistle to the Corinthians consists of thirteen chapters, 257 verses, and 6,092 words.

Situation

The second epistle to the Corinthians was written on Paul's third missionary journey a few months after 1 Corinthians. A date of AD 56 can be assigned to this epistle.

After writing 1 Corinthians, Paul traveled to Macedonia (Acts 20:1-2). There he met Titus who was returning from Corinth. Titus brought Paul good news (2 Corinthians 2:12f; 7:6f) and bad news about the situation in Corinth. On the one hand, the Corinthians had responded positively to the directions that Paul had given them in the first letter (2 Corinthians 7:5-15). The bad news was that some in Corinth were attacking Paul's credentials as an apostle. From Macedonia Paul wrote his second encounter epistle to the Corinthians.

Plan

The theme of 2 Corinthians is the *Defense of the Apostle*. Throughout the book Paul defends his conduct, character, and calling as an Apostle of Jesus Christ. In Romans Paul reveals his mind, in Galatians, his ire, in 1 Corinthians, his tact, and in 2 Corinthians, his heart. The following chart summarizes the criticisms of Paul, and the Apostle's response to them.

Corinthian Attack on Paul	
Their Attacks	**Paul's Response**
1. Paul is a self-appointed apostle.	1. When I was with you I worked all the powerful miracles, signs and wonders of a true apostle (2 Cor 12:12).
2. Paul is self-promoting.	2. We are not preaching about ourselves. Our message is that Jesus is Lord (2 Cor 4:5).
3. Paul can't be trusted, since he didn't come to Corinth when he said he would.	3. His last visit was so painful he had decided that a cooling off period was needed (2 Cor 2:1, 4).
4. Paul is pocketing money collected for poor saints.	4. We do not peddle the word of God for profit (2 Cor 2:17); Paul had refused to accept donations for himself (2 Cor 12:13), but had worked to support himself (Acts 18:3).
5. Paul's bark is stronger than his bite (2 Cor 10:10).	5. When I am with you, I will do exactly what I say in my letters (2 Cor 10:11).

Structural plan. Following a brief introduction, 2 Corinthians is organized into three major divisions. These are followed by a brief conclusion. The outline looks like this:

- **Introduction** (1:1-2)
- **Description of Paul's Ministry** (1:3–7:16)
- **Instruction about Paul's Collection** (chs. 8–9)
- **Vindication of Paul's Apostleship** (10:1–13:10)
- **Conclusion** (13:11-14)

Biographical plan. Aside from Christ, Paul the writer is the main focus of 2 Corinthians. Paul's lieutenant *Titus* is mentioned ten times in the book. He had been sent to Corinth to check up on how the Corinthians were responding to Paul's first letter. He rendezvoused with Paul in Macedonia, bringing a mixed report about the conditions in the church. *Timothy*, another key associate of Paul, is mentioned twice. Timothy and *Silas* (Silvanus) had preached for a time in Corinth along with Paul. The epistle also references two Old Testament characters: *Moses* and *Eve*.

Geographical plan. As might be expected, this epistle references the two regions of Greece. *Achaia (uh-khay'-iuh)* — the southern region where Corinth was located — is mentioned three times. *Macedonia (mas-eh-doh'-nih-aw)* — northern Greece from which Paul wrote the letter — is mentioned four times. Paul also noted that he was carrying an offering for the poor saints in *Judea* (2 Corinthians 1:16). Obviously the city of *Corinth* is mentioned. Paul also references *Troas* where he was supposed to meet Titus, but did not (2 Corinthians 2:12); and *Damascus* where Paul narrowly escaped arrest early in his ministry (2 Corinthians 11:32).

Eternal Purpose

The immediate purpose of 2 Corinthians is to express Paul's thanksgiving for the repentant majority in Corinth and to appeal to the rebellious minority to accept his apostolic authority. The deeper purpose of the book is to challenge every Christian to be an ambassador for Christ and to find consolation for all consequent suffering in the Lord.

1 & 2 Corinthians

A synopsis of 2 Corinthians is this: Paul defends his character, attitude, and teaching. He also promotes the collection for poor saints in Judea (chs. 8–9). A basic truth derived from this book is this: we find in Christ strength for every time of testing (7:7; 12:9).

The second letter to the Corinthians makes some important doctrinal contributions to the Bible. In this letter Paul contrasts the old and the new covenants (ch. 3), exposes the strategies of Satan (2:10-11; 4:4; 11:3, 13-15; 12:7), and gives a refreshing perspective on suffering for Christ (4:8-18). There are new insights in this book on the resurrection and judgment of Christians (5:1-13) and on the ministry of reconciliation (5:14-21). The apostle also emphasizes the importance of separation from the ways of the world (6:14–7:1).

Acclaim

In 2 Corinthians Paul presents Christ as the believer's triumph (2:14), Lord (4:5), light (4:6), judge (5:10), reconciler (5:19), substitute (5:21), indescribable gift (9:15), Master (10:7), and power (12:9). Perhaps the most distinctive portrait of Jesus in this book is the ***Comforter*** (1:5).

Keys

The key chapters in 2 Corinthians are chapters 8–9. These chapters contain the most complete revelation of God's plan for Christian giving found in the New Testament.

The key verse in the book is this: *We are therefore Christ's ambassadors, as though God were making his appeal through us. We implore you on Christ's behalf: Be reconciled to God* (5:20).

The key phrase in 2 Corinthians is *when I come* (4).

Key words include first person pronouns such as *I, we, us, our, my* (450 times), *grace* (12), and *brothers* (8).

Special Features

Here are some things that set 2 Corinthians apart from the other books of the New Testament.

- ❖ 2 Corinthians is full of autobiographical material — details about Paul's life that would otherwise be unknown.

- The language of 2 Corinthians is characterized by unusual constructions, broken sentences, mixed metaphors, and sudden shifts in feeling and tone.
- 2 Corinthians is the most unsystematic of Paul's writings. He frequently gives way to digressions.
- Bible scholars refer to 11:16–12:13 as Paul's Fool's Speech. It is a parody on ancient speeches and letters that commend a person.

HEAR

In addition to the key chapters referenced above, two other chapters in 2 Corinthians are outstanding:
- The future life (2 Corinthians 5)
- Paul's visions and revelations (2 Corinthians 12)

Some of the favorite lines in 2 Corinthians are these:
- *God loves a cheerful giver* (9:7).
- *A thorn in my flesh* (12:7).
- *To be away from the body and at home with the Lord* (5:8).
- *Though he was rich, yet for your sakes he became poor, so that you through his poverty might become rich* (8:9).
- *Thanks be to God for his indescribable gift* (9:15).
- *Do not be yoked together with unbelievers* (6:14).
- *If anyone is in Christ, he is a new creation; the old has gone, the new has come* (5:17).

CHAPTER SEVEN

ECCLESIA EPISTLES
Ephesians–Colossians

In this chapter we will survey three of the so-called *Prison Epistles* of Paul. The fourth epistle of this group was written to an individual. It will be taken up later. The letters to the Ephesians, Philippians, and Colossians were written by Paul from his first imprisonment in Rome. Because of the emphasis on the church in this trio of letters some refer to them as Paul's *ecclesia epistles*. *Ecclesia* in the Greek language means "called out ones." This is the regular Greek term translated *church* in the New Testament.

Each of these epistles has its own emphasis in the teaching about the church. If the church is a body, then Christ is the head. There is a living union between the two (Ephesians). If the church is a bride, then Christ is the bridegroom (Colossians). The union between Christ and his church is a loving one. If the church is a building—a temple—then Christ is the foundation. The union between Christ and his church is lasting (Philippians).

49th Book of the Bible
Book of Ephesians
Unity of Faith

Ephesians is the fifth epistle of Paul in the New Testament. After reading 1, 2 Corinthians and Galatians, this epistle comes as a pleasant surprise. Paul does not scold anyone, correct twisted theology, or defend himself against the attacks of his critics. Instead, Paul aims to enlarge the minds of his readers. He wants them to fully appreciate their standing in Christ.

The Epistle called Ephesians contains six chapters, 155 verses, and 3,039 words.

Situation

Paul spent two years in custody in Caesarea on the coast of Palestine. During that time he appeared before two Roman governors. Both men knew that Paul was not guilty of any capital crime. Yet both politicians wanted to please the Jewish religious establishment. Finally, Paul exercised his rights as a Roman citizen to appeal his case to the Emperor in Rome. Governor Festus had no choice but to arrange for Paul to be transported to Rome.

The voyage to Rome was harrowing. The ship sailed into a hurricane. It eventually ran aground and broke up off the shore of the island of Malta. Not one of the 276 passengers on board the ship was lost.

After wintering on the island of Malta, another vessel transported Paul to Italy. He and his guards and companions walked the last miles to the capital.

In Rome Paul was permitted to dwell by himself with the soldier who guarded him. He met with local Jewish and Christian leaders to explain why he had come to Rome as a prisoner. For two years he remained under house arrest (Acts 28:30). It was during this time that Paul penned the epistles called Ephesians, Philippians, Colossians as well as a personal letter to Philemon. A date of AD 62 or 63 is appropriate for these epistles.

At the same time that Paul wrote Colossians he wrote an epistle to the church at Laodicea (Colossians 4:16) ten miles to the west. Either this epistle has been lost, or we know it under a different name. Some think that the epistle we call *Ephesians* was originally sent to Laodicea. It then circulated among the churches in that region, winding up in Ephesus.

Plan

The style of Ephesians has been described as formal and impersonal. The subject matter is noncontroversial.

Structural plan. Ephesians has two main divisions sandwiched between a brief introduction and conclusion. The outline of Ephesians looks like this:

- ❖ **Introduction** (1:1-3)
- ❖ **Believer's Wealth in Christ** (1:4-3:21)
- ❖ **Believer's Walk in the World** (4:1-6:20)
- ❖ **Conclusion** (6:21-24)

The first main division focuses on how the Christian is blessed, saved, unified with other believers, and enlightened through the gospel. This doctrinal section of the book is interrupted by two prayers, one emphasizing knowledge (1:15-23), the other love (3:14-21).

The second main division of the epistle focuses on the believer's walk in the world. The Christian's walk must be worthy, different, loving, wise, and militant.

Biographical plan. Paul the writer of the letter was presently imprisoned for his commitment to Christ. Paul mentions only one associate, **Tychicus**. He probably delivered the epistle to its destination.

Geographical plan. The phrase *in Ephesus* (1:1) is missing in some ancient manuscripts. Some think this epistle was not specifically addressed to the church at Ephesus. It was intended as a circular letter for all the churches in the Lycus Valley. A main Roman road connected these cities to Ephesus. The epistle, however, eventually found a permanent home in Ephesus, hence came to be known as Ephesians.

Ephesus was located on the west coast of Asia Minor (modern Turkey), approximately three hundred miles due east of Corinth. The city was a great commercial center, ranking with Antioch and

Alexandria as one of the three greatest trading centers in the eastern Mediterranean. The chief attraction in the city was the temple to the goddess Diana (Artemis). Its magnificence was reported throughout the ancient world. Paul spent nearly three years in this city. His preaching had a profound impact on the Ephesians. Significant inroads against the worship of the local deity were made.

Eternal Purpose

Unlike the other Pauline epistles, Ephesians offers no clear explanation for its purpose in being composed. We can speculate that the immediate purpose of this epistle was to prevent problems in the church as a whole by encouraging the body of Christ to mature in him. The deeper purpose was to make believers aware of their position in Christ and the glory of Christ's body, the church.

Ephesians in synopsis is this: Paul first expounds the doctrine of our unity in Christ (chs. 1–3). He then indicates to all believers and to specific groups of believers practical steps for ensuring that this unity is maintained.

The fundamental truth set forth in this epistle is this: Christians are united in one Lord, one faith, and one baptism.

Acclaim

In Ephesians Paul paints a picture of Christ as *the **Head*** of the body or church. It was God's plan to bring all things in heaven and on earth together under one head, even Christ (1:10). God placed all things under his feet. He has appointed him to be head over everything for the church (1:22). A husband is the head of his wife; so Christ is the head of the church of which he is the Savior (5:23). Paul does not want his readers any longer to be infants tossed to and fro by every wind of doctrine. He wants them to grow up into him who is the head, even Christ (4:15).

Keys

The key chapter in Ephesians is chapter 6. In this chapter Paul makes clear that those who have been blessed in Christ must also battle against evil.

Ephesians–Colossians

The key verse in this book is this: *God placed all things under his [Christ's] feet and appointed him to be head over everything for the church, which is his body . . .* (Ephesians 1:22-23).

The key phrase, *in Christ* (or its equivalents), appears thirty-five times, more than in any other New Testament book.

Key words include *spirit* (15), *grace* (12), *body* (9), and *church* (9).

Special Features

Here are some facts about Ephesians that make it stand out in the biblical collection.

- ❖ Ephesians contains no personal greetings, nor does it identify any specific problems or controversies in the church.
- ❖ Paul communicates almost nothing about himself in Ephesians except the fact of his imprisonment.
- ❖ Ephesians contains forty-two words that occur nowhere else in the New Testament, and thirty-nine others that occur nowhere else in Paul's epistles.
- ❖ There is a striking similarity between Ephesians and Colossians. Seventy-eight out of 155 verses are identical or nearly identical.

HEAR

Aside from chapter 6 (see above), Ephesians 4, the great unity chapter, is a good sample of what Ephesians has to offer. Here are some favorite lines in the book:

- ❖ *Do not let the sun go down while you are still angry* (4:26).
- ❖ *Husbands, love your wives, just as Christ loved the church and gave himself up for her* (5:25).
- ❖ *For our struggle is not against flesh and blood, but against the rulers, against the authorities, against the powers of this dark world and against the spiritual forces of evil in the heavenly realms* (6:12).
- ❖ *Put on the full armor of God so that you can take your stand against the devil's schemes* (6:11).

- *For it is by grace you have been saved, through faith — and this not from yourselves, it is the gift of God — not by works, so that no one can boast (2:8-9).*
- *Do not get drunk on wine, which leads to debauchery. Instead, be filled with the Spirit (5:18).*

50th Book of the Bible
Book of Philippians
Joy in Christ

The fiftieth book of the Bible is called Philippians because it was sent to the congregation of Christians in the Macedonian city of Philippi. This is the sixth letter in our New Testament that was written by the Apostle Paul.

The Epistle to the Philippians contains four chapters, 104 verses and 2,002 words.

Situation

A date of about AD 63 is appropriate for Philippians.

On his second missionary journey Paul had a vision in which he saw a man from Macedonia beckoning him to come over into Europe to share the gospel. Paul answered the Macedonian call by traveling to Philippi (Acts 16:9).

Philippi was the first European city to be evangelized. It was also the first city to hear a gospel concert! After Paul and Silas were beaten and put in prison, they sang songs at midnight. Paul's stay in Philippi was crowned by three notable conversions: a businesswoman named Lydia, a soothsayer, and a jailer. The "we" passages in Acts suggest that Luke, the writer of Acts, was left in the city as the first minister of the church.

On his third missionary journey Paul passed through Philippi again (Acts 20:1, 6) en route to Corinth.

For the background of Philippians, see under Ephesians.

Plan

Philippians is a warm and informal letter. Paul's expressions of affection for the believers in Philippi exceed anything he said about the other churches to which he wrote. One can probably conclude that the congregation at Philippi was Paul's favorite. He called his readers *my dear friends* (2:12) and *my brothers* (4:1). There were no heart-wrenching problems of doctrine, discipline, or disorder over which he agonized as in his epistles to other congregations.

Structural plan. Like most informal letters, Philippians abruptly shifts from topic to topic. It is clear that Paul was not following strictly a predetermined outline. Even so the epistle to the Philippians breaks down into three major sections:

- **Personal Update** (1:1-26)
- **Passionate Appeals** (1:27–4:19)
- **Parting Words** (4:20-23)

Clearly the middle section of this Epistle is the "meat." In this section Paul urges his readers to have the patience (1:27-30), the mind (2:1-30), the knowledge (3:1-21), and the peace of Christ (4:1-19).

Biographical plan. Of course Paul speaks about himself in this letter, offering his readers an update on his situation in Rome. Paul mentions three of his associates as well. *Timothy* is mentioned along with Paul in the salutation of the epistle (1:1), probably because the Philippians knew him well. He had been with Paul in that city on the second missionary journey. *Timothy* is commended for having served Paul as a son serves his beloved father (2:22). Paul hoped to send Timothy to Philippi soon (2:19).

Paul mentions ***Epaphroditus*** (*e-paf'-roh-di'-tuhs*) twice. He was the messenger by whom the Philippians sent gifts to Paul during his first Roman imprisonment (2:25; 4:18). Epaphroditus had become seriously ill while in Rome. Paul urges the congregation at Philippi to receive him back with gladness (2:29).

Clement (*klehm'-uhnt*) is singled out among those in Philippi who are designated Paul's "fellow workers" (4:3). Nothing further is known about Clement.

Paul appeals for unity between two women—***Euodia*** (*u-oh'-de-ah*) and ***Syntyche*** (*sihn'-tih-khee*)—who apparently were rivals in the congregation at Philippi (4:2).

Geographical plan. Philippi was founded by Philip of Macedon, the father of Alexander the Great. It was the leading city in the region of Macedonia. Near Philippi Mark Antony's army was defeated by Octavian (later Caesar Augustus). Thereafter the city was settled as a military colony with special citizenship privileges. The city was located on a major highway called the Egnatian Way. Strangers from many lands passed through Philippi (*fihl-ihp'-pi*).

Macedonia, the region in which Philippi was located, is mentioned once (4:15). Paul also references his time of ministry in ***Thessalonica*** (*thehs-suh-loh-ni'-kuh*) about seventy-five miles southeast of Philippi. The Philippians had sent Paul aid while he had ministered in that city (4:16).

Eternal Purpose

The immediate purpose of the Epistle to the Philippians is to thank the Christians for their help in Paul's hour of need and to encourage greater unity in the congregation. The deeper purpose is to establish the truth that real unity and joy are possible only in Christ.

A synopsis of Philippians looks like this: Paul expresses his Christian joy in thanksgiving (1:1-26). He encourages his readers to steadfastness (1:27-30), unity (2:1-2), humility (2:3-11), and purity (2:12-18). He then warns them concerning the Judaizing false teachers (3:1-16) and the worldly (3:17-4:1). The epistle concludes with exhortations and thank you notes (4:2-23).

The basic truth taught in this epistle is that we should pattern our lives after Christ.

Acclaim

Philippians is full of portraits of Christ. In chapter 1 Christ is our Life (1:21). In chapter 2 he is our Model (2:5). Chapter 3 pictures him as the Transformer who changes our lowly body that it may be conformed to his glorious body (3:21). In chapter 4 Christ is the Enabler who supplies power for believers to soar over the circumstances of life (4:13).

The small amount of doctrinal teaching in this book centers in the person, presence, and power of Christ. Above all, Christ is the **Exalted Servant** (Philippians 2). Though he was on equality with the Father, Christ emptied himself. He took upon himself the form of a servant. He became obedient unto death, even the death of the cross. Then, however, the Father exalted him. He was given a name that is above all names. This passage is known to students of the New Testament as the *kenosis* (*emptying*) passage (2:5-11). Without question this is the most important passage about Christ in the writings of Paul, perhaps even in the entire New Testament.

Keys

The key chapter in Philippians is chapter 2. This chapter contains the revelation of *kenosis*, the *emptying* of Christ, referenced above.

The key verse in the book is this: *Rejoice in the Lord always. I will say it again: Rejoice!* (4:4).

The key phrase is *in the Lord* or equivalents (19 times).

The key words are first person pronouns (120), *joy/rejoice* (16), *gospel* (9), and *attitude/mind* (7).

Special Features

Here are some things about the Epistle to the Philippians that make it special in the New Testament.

- ❖ Philippians was written about ten years after Paul's first visit to Philippi.
- ❖ Lydia, a wealthy business woman, was the first European convert to the gospel. She was a founding member of the church at Philippi. Philippians indicates that women were quite influential in the success of the gospel in that city.
- ❖ Philippi is the only church in the New Testament that is said to have had both bishops (overseers) and deacons in positions of leadership.

- There is no mention of the Old Testament Scriptures in Philippians.
- Initially Paul was summoned to the city of Philippi by a vision (Acts 16:9).

HEAR

Here are some favorite lines from the Book of Philippians:
- *At the name of Jesus every knee should bow (2:10).*
- *My God will meet all your needs according to his glorious riches in Christ Jesus (4:19).*
- *For to me, to live is Christ and to die is gain (1:21).*
- *Forgetting what is behind and straining toward what is ahead, I press on toward the goal to win the prize for which God has called me heavenward in Christ Jesus (3:13-14).*
- *Our citizenship is in heaven (3:20).*
- *The peace of God, which transcends all understanding, will guard your hearts and your minds in Christ Jesus (4:7).*

51st Book of the Bible
Book of Colossians
God in Christ

The fifty-first book of the Bible is called *Colossians* (*koh-lahs'-shuhns*) because it originally was a letter sent to the church at Colosse (*koh-lah'-see*) in what is modern Turkey. This is the seventh epistle by Paul in the New Testament.

The Epistle to the Colossians consists of four chapters, ninety-five verses, and 1,998 words.

Situation

A date of about AD 62 is appropriate for Colossians. On the city of Colosse, see below under *Plan*.

The exact origins of the church at Colosse are unknown. *Epaphras* (*ehp'-uh-fras*) was a Colossian (Colossians 1:7; 4:12). He may have been the one who evangelized this city. Paul does not seem to have visited the city before he wrote his letter (Colossians 1:4; 2:1). He may, however, have visited the city later. *Philemon (fi-leh'-muhn)* and his slave *Onesimus (oh-nehs'-ih-muhs)* lived there (Colossians 4:9; Philemon 10). In fact the church at Colosse appears to have met in the house of Philemon (Philemon 2).

Paul met and converted the slave Onesimus during his first Roman imprisonment. He was sending this slave back to his Christian master. At this time he wrote a personal note to Philemon to facilitate reconciliation between the master and his runaway slave. That note is found later in our New Testament under the name *Philemon*. Paul took the occasion of the return of the slave to pen this epistle to the congregation.

Plan

Structural plan. Like most of Paul's letters, Colossians has a short introduction and conclusion. The theme of the epistle is **Godhead in Christ.** The "meat" of the letter consists of three distinct parts which center around the theme of the Lordship of Christ. The first section can be described as doctrinal in nature, the second as polemical (defensive), and the third as practical. The outline looks like this:

- ❖ **Introduction** (1:1-2)
- ❖ **Lordship of Christ Expounded** (1:3-2:7)
- ❖ **Lordship of Christ Defended** (2:8-3:4)
- ❖ **Lordship of Christ Applied** (3:5-4:6)
- ❖ **Conclusion** (4:7-18)

Biographical plan. Next to Christ, Paul the writer of the letter is the central figure in the epistle. He is a prisoner in Rome. Paul mentions nine associates in the epistle. *Timothy* is mentioned along with Paul in the greetings of five other epistles (2 Corinthians, Philippians, 1 & 2 Thessalonians, Philemon). Only in three of Paul's epistles is Timothy not mentioned (Galatians, Ephesians, Titus). As a young man Timothy joined Paul on his second missionary journey. He was close to Paul during the third missionary journey and the first Roman imprisonment.

Epaphras is mentioned twice (1:7; 4:12). He seems to have been the minister of the congregation in Colosse.

Tychicus (*tihk'-ih-kuhs*) (4:7) may have carried this letter to the Colossians. This associate had traveled with Paul on his third missionary journey. Paul assured his readers that Tychicus would give them an update on the apostle's activities. Later Paul sent Tychicus on a mission to Ephesus (2 Timothy 4:12).

Onesimus is the slave Paul converted in Rome. The apostle refers to him as *our faithful and dear brother* (4:9). He too would have much to relate by word of mouth to his fellow Colossians.

Paul names five who send greetings to the Colossians. This implies that they too were with Paul in Rome. Presumably these five were known to at least some of the Colossians, but in what capacity is unclear. The first to send greetings is ***Aristarchus*** (*her-his-tahr'-khuhs*), a Macedonian Jewish Christian. He is first mentioned as a traveling companion of Paul. He was seized by an angry crowd in Ephesus (Acts 19:29). He next is mentioned as one of two representatives carrying a donation from the church in Thessalonica to the needy Christians in Jerusalem (Acts 20:4). He accompanied Paul on the harrowing sea voyage to Rome (Acts 27:2). Now Paul refers to Aristarchus as *my fellow prisoner* (Colossians 4:10), by which he probably means one who is standing by him in his Roman imprisonment.

The second greeter is ***Mark*** the cousin of Barnabas (4:10). Mark was a dropout on Paul's first missionary journey, a reject on the second. At the time this epistle was written Mark was back in the good graces of Paul. Paul refers to him as *a fellow worker* (Philemon 24). Nothing is known about the third greeter, ***Jesus Justus***, except that he was a Jewish Christian (4:11).

The fourth greeter is ***Luke.*** He is called *our dear friend* and *the doctor* (4:10). Luke had traveled with Paul on the second and third missionary journeys. He may have been Paul's personal physician.

The fifth greeter is ***Demas***. He is called *my fellow worker* (Philemon 24). Five years later when Paul wrote a letter to

Timothy, Demas had deserted the apostle *because he loved this world* (2 Timothy 4:10).

Two individuals are singled out for greetings in Colossians. The first is **Nympha** (*nihm'-faw*), a female Christian[1] who hosted a house-church (4:15). The second is **Archippus** (*ahr-khihp'-puhs*), a minister at Colosse who needed to take heed (4:17).

Geographical plan. Colosse was a minor city about one hundred miles east of Ephesus. It was located in the fertile Lycus Valley by a mountain pass on the road from Ephesus to Damascus. Apart from this letter, Colosse exerted almost no influence on early church history.

Two other nearby cities in the Lycus Valley are also mentioned in the book: **Laodicea** (*lay-ahd-ih-see'-uh*) and **Hierapolis** (*hi-uhr-ahp'-oh-lihs*). Both of these towns were noted for their textile industry.

Eternal Purpose

The immediate purpose of Colossians is to combat a threatening heresy that was devaluing Christ, and to encourage the Colossians to continue in the faith. The deeper purpose of the book is to show that Christ is preeminent—first and foremost in everything—and the Christian's life should reflect that priority. In fending off the false teaching that was infiltrating the church at Colosse, Paul sketches for us a bright, clear vision of Jesus Christ. Our Lord plays a central role not only in God's plan, but in our lives as well.

In synopsis Colossians reads like this: In Christ all the fullness of the godhead dwelled bodily (2:9, 10). Therefore, he is the focus of our faith. One must not be deceived by theologies or systems that detract from his preeminence. All believers should reflect in their conduct in the home and church their relationship with Christ.

Colossians expresses the basic truth that the Godhead was incarnate in Jesus.

---

[1] The KJV renders this name masculine "Nymphas" and renders "his house" in Colossians 4:15.

Acclaim

In Ephesians Paul portrayed the church of Christ. Now in Colossians he focuses on the Christ of the church. If Ephesians focuses on the Body, Colossians concentrates on the Head. The most significant characteristic of the book is its Christology — its teaching about Jesus. Christ is portrayed as the *Incarnate God.*

Colossians stresses the supremacy of Christ. He is superior to every principality and power — invisible spiritual beings of the angel class (2:10). Christ is the Lord of creation (1:16-17), the source of reconciliation (1:20-23; 2:13-15). The believer's hope is grounded in him (1:5, 23, 27). It is Christ that enables the believer to live the new life (1:11, 29). He is our Redeemer and Reconciler (1:14, 20-22; 2:11-15). In him is embodied the fullness of deity (1:15, 19; 2:9). He is in fact the Creator and Sustainer of all things (1:16-17). Because of his resurrection and ascension he is the Head of the church (1:18; 3:1), and the all sufficient Savior (1:28; 2:3, 10; 3:1-4).

Keys

The key chapter in Colossians is chapter 3. This chapter links the themes of Colossians together showing their cause-and-effect relationships.

The key verse in the book is this: *[Christ] is the image of the invisible God, the firstborn over all creation* (Colossians 1:15).

The key phrases are *with Christ* (3) and *put on* (3).

The key word in the book is *wisdom* (6).

Special Features

Here are a few of the features of Colossians that set it apart from the other books of Scripture.

- ❖ Seventy-eight of the ninety-five verses — about 82% — in Colossians are nearly identical to those in Ephesians.
- ❖ Colossians uses fifty-five Greek words that do not appear in Paul's other epistles, thirty-four of those occurring nowhere else in the New Testament.
- ❖ As in the case of Romans, this letter was written to a church Paul never had visited.

❖ There are no Old Testament references in this epistle.
❖ Colossians is perhaps the most Christ-centered book in the Bible.

HEAR

Here are some of the favorite lines from the Epistle to the Colossians:

❖ *Whatever you do, whether in word or deed, do it all in the name of the Lord Jesus, giving thanks to God the Father through him* (3:17).
❖ *Christ is all, and is in all* (3:11).
❖ *He has rescued us from the dominion of darkness and brought us into the kingdom of the Son he loves* (1:13).
❖ *In Christ all the fullness of the Deity lives in bodily form* (2:9).
❖ *Set your minds on things above, not on earthly things* (3:2).

Chapter Eight

ESCHATOLOGICAL EPISTLES
1 & 2 Thessalonians

The study of the events of the last days is called *eschatology*. The earliest of Paul's epistles emphasize events of the last days. So 1 & 2 Thessalonians are Paul's *eschatological epistles*.

In the evangelical epistles (Romans, Galatians) the emphasis is on *Christ and the cross*. Faith looks back to the cross and is strengthened. Believers are depicted raised up with Christ. In the encounter epistles (1 & 2 Corinthians) the theme is *Christ and the critics*. Faith looks down to the foundation and is measured. Believers are depicted contending for Christ. In the ecclesia epistles (Ephesians–Colossians) the theme is *Christ and the church*. Faith looks up to the bridegroom and is deepened. Believers are depicted seated with Christ. Now in the eschatological epistles the theme is *Christ and the coming*—the Second Coming—Christ's return to earth. Faith looks forward and is encouraged. Believers are depicted caught up to be with Christ.

52nd Book of the Bible
Book of 1 Thessalonians
Revelation of Christ

In some respects Paul's eighth epistle in the New Testament is similar to 2 Corinthians. In these pages Paul manifests his innermost feelings. His compassion, affection, and concern for the spiritual well-being of his converts shine through.

The first letter to the Thessalonians contains five chapters, eighty-nine verses, and 1,857 words.

Situation

The first letter to the Thessalonians was probably Paul's earliest epistle. A date of about AD 50 is appropriate.

Paul visited Thessalonica on his second missionary journey after he left Philippi. It was in this city that Paul's preaching attracted a numerous and socially prominent following (Acts 17:4). Unable to exert pressure on the public officials, Paul's Jewish opponents resorted to mob agitation to force the government's hand. The authorities took action to get rid of Paul with minimum hardship to him.

The new Christians sent away the missionaries (Paul, Silas, Timothy) by night. They moved down the road forty-five miles to Berea where they found a more sympathetic reception. When the agitators in Thessalonica heard that Paul was preaching in Berea, they traveled there. Again the agitators stirred up trouble against the missionaries. The new Christians in Berea sent Paul away to the nearest seaport. Paul sailed for Athens, leaving Silas and Timothy behind temporarily (Acts 17:1-15).

The first letter to the Thessalonians was written soon after Paul's departure from the area. This letter reflects Paul's anxiety to fortify his new converts from inroads by false teachers (2 Thessalonians 2:2) and from discouragement in the face of further persecution (1 Thessalonians 3:3).

Plan

Structural plan. After a brief introduction, 1 Thessalonians has five major divisions. The letter can be outlined like this:

- ❖ **Introduction** (1:1)
- ❖ **Commendation of the Church** (1:2-10)
- ❖ **Commencement of the Church** (2:1–3:10)
- ❖ **Concerns for the Church** (3:11–4:12)

❖ **Coming for the Church** (4:13–5:11)

❖ **Commands for the Church** (5:12-24)

The first main division speaks about how the gospel had impacted the Thessalonians. The second reviews how the gospel had come into the city of Thessalonica. The third division sets forth the areas in which the Thessalonians needed to grow. The fourth division develops the teaching about how Christ will come again. The last division deals with the practical issue of how Christians should live as they await the Second Coming of Christ.

Biographical plan. In 1 Thessalonians Paul reveals his pastoral concern for new converts. He names two associates, both of whom are mentioned alongside Paul as those who were sending this epistle. Paul had dispatched **Timothy** from Athens to work with the new Christians in Thessalonica (3:2). Timothy rejoined Paul at Corinth a few months later. He brought the apostle a positive report on the developments among the Christians in Thessalonica (3:6).

The other associate mentioned in the letter is **Silvanus** (*sihl-vay'-nuhs*). This is a Latin form of the Greek name *Silas*. He was a prophet in the Jerusalem church. One of his early assignments was to carry news of the Jerusalem conference to the believers at Antioch (Acts 15:22). Silas accompanied Paul on the second missionary journey. He and Paul traveled from Antioch through Asia Minor (Acts 15:40-41) and on into Macedonia in Europe. In Philippi the two were imprisoned (Acts 16:19-24). That night they led the jailer and his family to the Lord after God destroyed the prison in an earthquake. Later in his ministry Silas teamed with Peter on missions in Pontus and Cappadocia, Roman provinces located in what is today Turkey. Silas also served as Peter's scribe, writing 1 Peter and perhaps other letters.

Geographical plan. Thessalonica was the seaport capital of the Roman province of Macedonia (northern Greece). This prosperous city was located on the Via Egnatia, the main highway from Rome to Damascus. Thessalonica had a sizable Jewish population. The high moral standards and monotheism of Judaism attracted many prominent Gentiles in the city who had become disenchanted with Greek paganism. The city as a whole, however, had the kind of reputation that any large city frequented by sailors and traveling merchants might have today. Sexual immorality was commonplace.

Three regions are mentioned in the letter. The two major divisions of ancient Greece—*Macedonia* and *Achaia*—are mentioned together twice (1:7, 8). The positive reputation of the Thessalonian converts for Christian living and devotion to evangelism spread throughout that region (4:10). The only other region mentioned in the letter is *Judea*. The Christians in Thessalonica were suffering persecution just like the original Christians in Judea (Jerusalem area) had suffered before them.

Besides Thessalonica, only one other city is mentioned. Paul alludes to the persecution the missionaries had experienced in *Philippi* prior to coming to the city of Thessalonica (2:2).

Eternal Purpose

The immediate purpose of 1 Thessalonians is to express Paul's thanksgiving for the faith and love of these Christians and to encourage them in the midst of a local persecution. The deeper purpose of the epistle is to set forth vital truths concerning the *parousia* (presence) or Second Coming of Christ.

In synopsis form the letter looks like this: the Second Coming of Christ is the hope of the believer (1:9-10), the motivation for service (2:19-20), the basis of personal dedication (3:13), and the answer to many perplexing questions (4:13-18; 5:9).

The basic truth taught in this letter is that we must wait and watch for the Second Coming of Christ.

Acclaim

In 1 Thessalonians Paul paints a portrait of Jesus as the *Returning Son*. Paul sees Christ as the believer's hope of salvation both now and at his return. When Jesus returns, he will deliver (1:10; 5:4-11), reward (2:19), perfect (3:13), resurrect (4:13-18), and sanctify or make holy (5:23) all who trust him.

1 & 2 Thessalonians

Keys

The key chapter in 1 Thessalonians is chapter 4. This chapter contains the central message of the epistle about the coming of the Lord Jesus.

The key verse is this: *You turned to God from idols to serve the living and true God, and to wait for his Son from heaven . . .* (1:9-10).

The key phrase is *from heaven* (2).

Key words include *love* (6), *comfort/comforted* (6), and *coming* (4).

Special Features

Some distinguishing facts about 1 Thessalonians are these:
- ❖ The apostle's great writing career begins with this letter.
- ❖ Each of the five chapters ends with a reference to the Lord's return.
- ❖ There are no quotes from the Old Testament in 1 Thessalonians.
- ❖ Speculation about the date of the "rapture" — the taking away of believers — is big business. Hal Lindsey's book *Late Great Planet Earth* (1976) sold eleven million copies. Four million copies of the booklet *88 Reasons Why the Rapture Will Be in 1988* by Edgar Whisenant were published. Sixteen volumes of the *Left Behind* series by authors Timothy LaHaye and Jerry Jenkins with spinoff movies and video games have made a significant impact on American culture.

HEAR

Here are some favorite lines from the first epistle to the Thessalonians:
- ❖ *The day of the Lord will come like a thief in the night* (5:2).
- ❖ *After that, we who are still alive and are left will be caught up together with them [the resurrected Christian dead] in the clouds to meet the Lord in the air. And so we will be with the Lord forever* (4:17).

- *Do not put out the Spirit's fire* (5:19)
- *Be joyful always; pray continually* (5:16-17).
- *Satan stopped us* (2:18).

53rd Book of the Bible
Book of 2 Thessalonians
Ruin of the World

We have now come to the last of the nine congregational epistles written by the Apostle Paul.

In 2 Thessalonians there are three chapters, forty-seven verses, and 1,042 words.

Situation

The second epistle to the Thessalonians was written in the year AD 50 a few months after 1 Thessalonians. A misunderstanding spawned by false teachers had arisen in the church at Thessalonica after they had received Paul's first letter. False teachers were saying that the day of the Lord—some spiritual return of Christ—already had come. Paul wanted his readers to know that despite reports to the contrary, the day of the Lord had not yet come. Certain events must first take place before the coming of the Lord.

Plan

Structural plan. The theme of 2 Thessalonians is *the ruin of the world*. Following a brief introduction the second epistle to the Thessalonians is organized into three main divisions. The outline looks like this:

- **Introduction** (1:1-4)
- **Purpose of Christ's Coming** (1:5-12)
- **Prerequisites of Christ's Coming** (2:1-12)
- **Preparation for Christ's Coming** (2:13–3:17)

Biographical plan. In this epistle Paul is the concerned pastor. He references two of his associates, both of whom were mentioned in the first epistle to this church. Paul's associates *Silvanus* or *Silas* and **Timothy** are mentioned alongside Paul as senders of the epistle (1:1).

Eternal Purpose

The second letter to the Thessalonians is the theological sequel to 1 Thessalonians, which introduced the theme of the coming day of the Lord. The immediate purpose of this epistle is to correct some misconceptions about the day of the Lord. The deeper purpose of 2 Thessalonians is to set forth how Christians must behave as they wait for the Lord's coming.

A synopsis of this short epistle looks like this: Believers can rest assured that Christ is coming to take vengeance on those who know not God and who obey not the Lord Jesus (1:7-8). Before the day of the Lord there will come a great falling away. The *man of sin* will be revealed (2:3). Believers must therefore stand fast (2:15).

So the basic truth of this epistle is that the church will face a great falling away before Christ comes.

The Thessalonian epistles are not doctrinal treatises like Romans and Ephesians. Yet these two epistles allude to almost every core doctrine of the Christian faith. The major contribution, however, is the doctrine of the day of the Lord. Paul insisted that the day of the Lord had not yet come in AD 50. Some Christian scholars think that the day of the Lord is the fall of Jerusalem and dispersion of the Jewish people in AD 70. Whereas this Jerusalem judgment may be *a* day of the Lord, *the* day of the Lord is connected with final judgment and the return of Christ. Obviously that day has not yet come. Before it comes there will be a falling away (2:3).

Commentators differ on their understanding of the falling away. Some think it refers to the departure from New Testament teaching that evolved over centuries into the Roman Catholic Church. Others think the falling away refers to what is called modernism—the denial of anything miraculous, including the Virgin Birth of Christ and his bodily resurrection.

The falling away will culminate in the revelation of one that Paul calls *the man of sin* or *lawlessness*. This man's appearance in the world demands the removal of the restrainer (2:6-7). Again there is much dispute about whom or what this man of sin is. Some say he represents the pope. Others think he is some evil dictator who has not yet appeared on the scene. The restrainer has been taken to be 1) the Roman Empire, 2) law and order, 3) Satan, or 4) the Holy Spirit.

Acclaim

In 2 Thessalonians Paul paints a portrait of the **Glorified Son**. For believers the return of Christ is a joyful prospect for which we yearn. His return from heaven, however, has fearful consequences for those who do not believe in Jesus (1:6-10; 2:8-12).

Keys

The key chapter in 2 Thessalonians is chapter 2. This chapter corrects a serious misunderstanding about the day of the Lord.

The key verse in the book is this: *stand firm and hold to the teachings we passed on to you . . .* (2:15).

The key phrase in the book is *the name of our Lord Jesus Christ* (2).

Key words include *day* (4), *revealed* (4), and *glorified* (3).

Special Features

Here are some of the unique features of 2 Thessalonians that set it apart within the sacred collection:

- ❖ 2 Thessalonians is the shortest of Paul's nine epistles to churches.
- ❖ 2 Thessalonians closes with a greeting in Paul's own hand (3:17).
- ❖ 2 Thessalonians was written from Corinth, the last location where Paul, Silas, and Timothy are known to have been together.
- ❖ Paul offers four prayers on behalf of the readers of this short epistle.

1 & 2 Thessalonians

HEAR

Here are some favorite lines from 2 Thessalonians:
- *For even when we were with you, we gave you this rule: "If a man will not work, he shall not eat" (3:10).*
- *. . . and give relief to you who are troubled, and to us as well. This will happen when the Lord Jesus is revealed from heaven in blazing fire with his powerful angels. He will punish those who do not know God and do not obey the gospel of our Lord Jesus (1:7-8).*
- *That day will not come until the rebellion occurs and the man of lawlessness is revealed, the man doomed to destruction (2:3).*
- *Keep away from every brother who is idle and does not live according to the teaching you received from us (3:6).*
- *Never tire of doing what is right (3:13).*

Chapter Nine

Letters to a Preacher
1 & 2 Timothy

In the previous four chapters we surveyed Paul's congregational epistles. In the next two chapters we will examine his personal and pastoral letters. These letters were written to three individuals: Timothy, Titus, and Philemon. The first two of these men were preachers of the gospel and Paul's associates. Philemon was a wealthy businessman whom Paul had converted. He was a member of the congregation that met at Colosse.

Because of their concerns about congregational issues, 1 & 2 Timothy and Titus are called Paul's *Pastoral Epistles*. Philemon is hard to classify. Chronologically it belongs with Colossians. Since, however, it is a letter to an individual, it was placed with the letters to Timothy and Titus in early Christian collections. Its position following the two Timothys and Titus is explained by the fact that it is the smallest of Paul's letters to individuals. Some designate the four epistles together as the *exhortation epistles*. The thrust of these four epistles is *Christ and the charge*, the watchword is *faithful to Christ*. In these four letters faith looks within the heart and is encouraged.

54th Book of the Bible
Book of 1 Timothy
Faithfulness in Christ

The first letter to Timothy is the first of Paul's personal or pastoral letters to appear in the New Testament, but not the first to be written. That distinction goes to the little letter to Philemon.

Paul's first letter to Timothy contains six chapters, 113 verses, and 2,269 words.

Situation

At the close of the Book of Acts Paul was under house arrest in Rome. He was waiting for his hearing before the Emperor Nero. Paul waited two years for his accusers to show up from Judea. Apparently they never came. Roman law required a case to be dismissed when there was no prosecution after two years. Paul must have been released from custody as he anticipated he would be in Philippians 1:19, 25, 26; 2:24.

After Paul's release from Roman prison in ca. AD 63 he traveled about in further missionary activity. While traveling through Macedonia he wrote the first epistle to Timothy. At the time Timothy was serving as Paul's representative in Ephesus. A date of about AD 65 is appropriate for this letter.

Plan

Structural plan. The theme of 1 Timothy is *the charge concerning faithfulness*. The book contains the charge or challenge of a senior minister to a younger evangelist. The first epistle to Timothy is organized into four divisions. The outline of the epistle looks like this:

- ❖ **Pure Doctrine** (ch. 1)
- ❖ **Public Worship** (chs. 2–3)
- ❖ **Perverted Teaching** (ch. 4)
- ❖ **Pastoral Duties** (chs. 5–6)

Biographical plan. The recipient of this letter is mentioned three times in the book. He is mentioned a total of twenty-four times in the New Testament. Timothy was from Lystra. He was probably converted on Paul's first journey. His mother and grandmother were godly Jewish women, but his father was a pagan Greek (Acts 16:1-2).

Timothy joined Paul, Silas, and Luke on the second missionary journey. He was circumcised by Paul so he could preach the gospel in Jewish synagogues. Timothy also accompanied Paul on the third missionary journey. He stayed close to Paul during his first Roman imprisonment (Philippians 1:1; Colossians 1:1; Philemon 1). Timothy performed ministry in at least five churches: Thessalonica (1 Thessalonians 3:2, 6), Corinth (1 Corinthians 4:17; 2 Corinthians 1:19), Philippi (Philippians 2:19-23), Berea (Acts 17:14), and Ephesus (1 Timothy 1:3).

Two other believers are mentioned in the first epistle to Timothy. **Hymenaeus** (*hee'-meh-nee'-uhs*) and **Alexander** had become shipwrecked concerning the faith. The problem with Hymenaeus had to do with doctrine. He taught that the resurrection already had occurred (2 Timothy 2:17-18). Presumably Alexander was also a false prophet. Whether he is to be identified with Alexander the coppersmith (2 Timothy 4:14) is disputed. Paul delivered these men to Satan—excommunicated them—so that they would not be able any longer to corrupt the believers.

Two Old Testament characters—*Adam* and *Eve*—are mentioned in 1 Timothy. Paul refers to the original relationship between our first parents in order to explain the relationship between men and women in the teaching ministry of the church (1 Timothy 2:13f).

In this epistle Paul also refers to **Pontius Pilate** before whom Christ gave his testimony (6:13).

Geographical plan. In 1 Timothy Paul mentions the city of **Ephesus** (1:3). Paul left Timothy to minister in this great city when he departed for **Macedonia** (northern Greece). It was from Macedonia that Paul wrote this letter to Timothy.

Eternal Purpose

The immediate purpose of 1 Timothy is to encourage and exhort the young minister concerning both his personal and public life. The ultimate purpose of this letter is to provide the church with a leadership manual.

A synopsis of 1 Timothy looks like this: Paul gives directions for public worship and for the proper organization of the church, including the qualifications of elders and deacons.

The basic truth taught in this epistle is that we should behave in the house of God (the church body).

Personal letters like 1 Timothy assume rather than set forth New Testament doctrine. This epistle is primarily concerned with the application of Christian truth in individual and congregational life. This letter is rich in principles that are relevant to every Christian worker and Christian church. Paul concentrates mostly on two areas. Timothy is to urge the churches to maintain purity of doctrine and lifestyle.

Acclaim

In 1 Timothy Christ is recognized as God manifested in the flesh. Paul pens lines that sound very much like an early Christian confession: *[Christ] was vindicated by the Spirit, was seen by angels, was preached among the nations, was believed on in the world, was taken up in glory* (3:16). Christ is the source of spiritual strength (1:12). Grace, faith, and love can be experienced through him (1:14). Christ came into the world to save sinners (1:15). He gave himself a ransom for all (2:6). He is the Savior of all men, especially of those who believe (4:10). In 1 Timothy Christ is the one Mediator between God and men (2:5). The picture, however, that we will associate with 1 Timothy is that Christ is the *Eternal, Immortal, Invisible King* (1 Timothy 1:17).

Keys

The key chapter in 1 Timothy is chapter 3. This is the chapter that contains the qualifications for the leaders of God's church.

1 & 2 Timothy

The key verse in the book is this: *I am writing you these instructions so that . . . you will know how people ought to conduct themselves in God's household . . .* (1 Timothy 3:14-15).

The key phrases are *trustworthy saying* (3) and *the faith* (7).

Key words include *faith* (19), *charge* (6), and *law* (3).

Special Features

Here are the special features of 1 Timothy that make it stand out among the biblical books:

- ❖ The most explicit directions for church leadership and organization in the Bible are found in 1 Timothy.
- ❖ One of the best refutations of the "health and wealth" gospel is found in 1 Timothy 6.

HEAR

Below are some key lines from the first epistle to Timothy:
- ❖ *The love of money is a root of all kinds of evil* (6:10).
- ❖ *Christ Jesus came into the world to save sinners — of whom I am the worst* (1:15).
- ❖ *There is one God and one mediator between God and men, the man Christ Jesus, who gave himself as a ransom for all men* (2:5-6).
- ❖ *The Spirit clearly says that in later times some will abandon the faith and follow deceiving spirits and things taught by demons* (4:1).
- ❖ *If anyone does not provide for his relatives, and especially for his immediate family, he has denied the faith and is worse than an unbeliever* (5:8).
- ❖ *We brought nothing into the world, and we can take nothing out of it* (6:7).
- ❖ *Fight the good fight of the faith* (6:12).

55th Book of the Bible
Book of 2 Timothy
Soundness in Christ

Chronologically 2 Timothy is the last of the thirteen epistles attributed to Paul. The last words of a famous person — whether intentional or unintentional — often reveal character and purpose. The second letter to Timothy contains the last known words of the great Apostle Paul. These final words to a young evangelist are as relevant today as the day they were written. If we as believers embrace the values of this epistle, our lives will be enriched beyond measure.

The second letter to Timothy has been characterized as a "combat manual" and Paul's "last will and testament." Here Paul evaluates God's past dealings with him, analyzes his present situation, and anticipates his imminent departure to enter the celestial kingdom.

The second epistle to Timothy contains four chapters, eighty-three verses, and 1,703 words.

Situation

Paul was rearrested in Rome about AD 66 and subsequently executed in AD 67 or earlier AD 68. This was during the reign of the Emperor Nero. During this second imprisonment Paul wrote his last epistle. The earlier Prison Epistles (Ephesians, Philippians, Colossians, Philemon) were written from the relative comfort of house arrest. When he writes 2 Timothy, Paul languishes in a cold dungeon, chained like a dangerous criminal.

Plan

The second letter to Timothy develops the theme of *the preacher and the word*. The four chapters of the book indicate the four main points of emphasis which can be set forth in an appealing alliterative outline: power, preservation, protection, and proclamation of the gospel. Another outline using action words looks like this:

❖ **Embrace the Word** (ch. 1)
❖ **Teach the Word** (ch. 2)
❖ **Defend the Word** (ch. 3)
❖ **Preach the Word** (ch. 4)

Biographical plan. As might be expected, in his second letter to Timothy Paul speaks a great deal about himself. He depicts himself as a traveling minister who has started churches throughout the Roman Empire. Paul also mentions twenty-three men, women, friends, and foes, many of whom are mentioned only here in the Bible.

Timothy was one of Paul's most devoted traveling companions. Paul had appointed him to lead the church in Ephesus.

Three who did injury to Paul are named: ***Alexander*** the coppersmith (4:14). Paul says that this man, whoever he was, had done him great harm. Presumably he lived in Ephesus. ***Phygelus*** (*fih-ghehl'-us*) and ***Hermogenes*** (*huhr-mohgh'-ih-nees*) (1:15) are singled out among those who had turned away from Paul.

Two in particular are named as those who had aided Paul. ***Carpus*** lived in Troas on the coast of Asia (modern day Turkey). Paul had left his cloak with him. ***Onesiphorus*** (*oh-neh-sihf'-oh-ruhs*) had often refreshed Paul (1:16). He was not ashamed of Paul's chains or imprisonment.

Besides Timothy, eight of Paul's ministerial associates are named. ***Tychicus*** (4:12) had been sent to Ephesus, presumably as Timothy's replacement. Timothy was told to get ***Mark*** and bring him to Rome. Paul states that Mark was *useful to me for ministering* (4:11). ***Luke*** was the only associate remaining with Paul at the time he wrote 2 Timothy (4:11). ***Titus*** (4:10) had been sent to Dalmatia, the region of modern Albania and Slovenia. ***Crescens*** (4:10) had been sent to Galatia, in the heartland of modern Turkey. ***Demas*** (4:10) had forsaken Paul and gone to Thessalonica. ***Erastus*** (4:20) had remained at Corinth. He may be the same as the Erastus who had once worked with Timothy in Macedonia (Acts 19:22) and the Erastus who was the director of public works in Corinth (Romans 16:23). Paul had left **Trophimus** (*trahf'-ih-muhs*) (4:20) at Miletus sick.

Timothy was told to salute three individuals or groups in Ephesus. Paul's good friends **Prisca** (Priscilla) and **Aquila** had returned to Ephesus from Rome where we last heard of them (Romans 16:3). Timothy was also to greet the *household of Onesiphorus* (4:19), the gentleman mentioned previously in 1:16.

Four are named that sent greetings to Timothy: **Eubulus, Pudens, Linus,** and **Claudia**. Nothing further is known about these four.

Two false teachers are named. **Hymaeneus** (*hee'-meh-nee'-uhs*) and **Philetus** (*fih-lee'-tuhs*) (2:17) held to the belief that the resurrection is past. They denied a future bodily resurrection, claiming that the only resurrection that we experience is the spiritual resurrection of our new birth. The first of these false teachers was named in 1 Timothy 1:20. He had been excommunicated from the church by Paul for blasphemy (speaking against God). Apparently he continued to spread his false doctrine even after his expulsion from the church.

Paul alludes to two female relatives of Timothy: **Lois** was Timothy's grandmother, **Eunice** was his mother (1:5). Both were godly women who passed down their love for God to Timothy.

Paul alludes to Old Testament **David** as an ancestor of Christ (2:8). He also mentions the names of two otherwise unknown Egyptian magicians who confronted Moses (3:8).

Geographical plan. In 2 Timothy Paul mentions three regions where the work of the gospel was going forward. He alludes to the Roman provinces of **Asia** and **Galatia** in what is today Turkey. He also makes mention of **Dalmatia**, the region north of Greece, modern Albania or Slovenia.

Nine cities are mentioned in the book. Of course there is reference to **Rome** (1:17) where Paul was in prison and **Ephesus** (1:18; 4:12) where Timothy ministered. Three cities where Paul was persecuted are named: **Antioch, Iconium,** and **Lystra** (3:11). These cities were located in what is today the country of Turkey. Paul mentions **Thessalonica** in Macedonia as the destination of Demas.

Paul mentions having left his cloak in the city of **Troas** on the coast of what is today Turkey. **Corinth** is mentioned as the city where Erastus remained. **Miletus,** another coastal city in what is today Turkey, is where Paul left Trophimus who had fallen sick.

Eternal Purpose

The immediate purpose of Paul's second letter to Timothy is to encourage the young evangelist in the hardships he was facing. The deeper purpose is to encourage Christian leaders to be bold in the proclamation of the gospel.

A synopsis of 2 Timothy looks like this: Paul urges Timothy to hold on to the faith, teach it, abide in it, and preach it.

The basic truth in this book is that we must endure hardship as a good soldier.

Acclaim

The doctrine of Christ is not the major focus of 2 Timothy. Nonetheless, choice statements are made about our Lord in this epistle. Christ Jesus appeared on earth. He abolished death and brought life and immortality to light through the gospel (1:10). Christ rose from the dead (2:8). He provides *salvation* and *eternal glory* (2:10) to those who put their hope in him. We who have *died with him* will *also live with him* (2:11). Those who are faithful until death will *reign with him* (2:12). When he appears the second time, we will receive the *crown of righteousness* (4:8).

The lasting portrait of Jesus that we will associate with the second letter to Timothy is **Faithful Friend** (4:17). He is the one who always stands by our side.

Keys

The key chapter in 2 Timothy is chapter 2. In this chapter Paul lists the fundamentals of a successful ministry.

The key verse is this: *The things you have heard me say in the presence of many witnesses entrust to reliable men who will also be qualified to teach others* (2 Timothy 2:2).

The key phrase is *shall be* (5).

Key words include *know* (6) and *life* (5).

Special Features

Here are some of the special considerations that set 2 Timothy apart within the sacred collection.

- ❖ This book has provided comfort, encouragement, and motivation to distressed Christian workers over the centuries.
- ❖ This is Paul's most personal letter. In Romans we see Paul the theologian; in 1 Corinthians, Paul the counselor; in 2 Corinthians, Paul the preacher; in Galatians, Paul the defender; in 1 Timothy and Titus, Paul the statesman; but in 2 Timothy, Paul the *man*.
- ❖ 2 Timothy contains Paul's last known request (4:9). He wants Timothy to travel a thousand miles over land and sea to come to him. He wants to die in the company of those he loves.
- ❖ Timothy's name is found more often in the salutations of the Pauline Epistles than any other.
- ❖ 2 Timothy contains two important prophecies about coming conditions of apostasy: empty profession and spiritual deception (3:1-9; 4:3-4).
- ❖ Here only in sacred literature does one find the names of two of the Egyptian magicians who opposed Moses (3:8): Jannes and Jambres.

HEAR

In addition to the key verse, some of the favorite lines in 2 Timothy are these:

- ❖ *I have fought the good fight, I have finished the race, I have kept the faith* (4:7).
- ❖ *Fan into flame the gift of God, which is in you* (1:6).
- ❖ *Do your best to present yourself to God as one approved, a workman who does not need to be ashamed and who correctly handles the word of truth* (2:15).
- ❖ *All Scripture is God-breathed and is useful for teaching, rebuking, correcting and training in righteousness, so that*

the man of God may be thoroughly equipped for every good work (3:16-17).
❖ *Preach the Word; be prepared in season and out of season; correct, rebuke and encourage — with great patience and careful instruction* (4:2).
❖ *The Lord stood at my side and gave me strength* (4:17).

Chapter Ten

Letters to an Associate and a Friend
Titus & Philemon

In the previous chapter we surveyed the first two of the exhortation epistles. In this chapter we will examine the final two books of this quartet.

56th Book of the Bible
Book of Titus
Steadfastness in Christ

The two letters to Timothy and Titus are letters to Paul's younger associates who were ministering in various areas. For this reason these books are called Paul's *Pastoral Epistles*. Compared to the Timothy correspondence, the Titus letter displays a different focus. In the two Timothys Paul addresses *doctrine*; in Titus the focus is more on *duty*. Broken down individually, 1 Timothy emphasizes the *protection* of the gospel, 2 Timothy the *proclamation* of the gospel, and Titus the *practice* of the gospel.

Titus is similar to 1 Timothy in date, circumstances, and purpose. Both are full of encouragement and exhortation. There is this difference. Titus is briefer, more official, and less personal than 1 Timothy. Timothy's situation at Ephesus required a stronger emphasis on sound doctrine, while Titus's situation at Crete required a greater focus on conduct. In essence this letter is a veteran missionary's advice to a younger minister.

The Book of Titus contains three chapters, forty-six verses, and 921 words.

Situation

Titus accompanied Paul to Crete subsequent to Paul's release from his first Roman imprisonment (AD 64). He was left there to consolidate the work (Titus 1:5f). Paul penned the letter to Titus to notify him that he would be relieved on Crete by Artemas or Tychicus (Titus 3:12).

Plan

Structural plan. The letter to Titus emphasizes *steadfastness in Christ*. The book has three major divisions sandwiched between a brief introduction and conclusion. The three main divisions focus on protecting, proclaiming, and practicing sound doctrine. The outline looks like this:

- ❖ **Introduction** (1:1-4)
- ❖ **Mission of Titus** (1:5-16)
- ❖ **Message of Titus** (2:1-15)
- ❖ **Manner of Titus** (3:1-11)
- ❖ **Conclusion** (3:12-15)

Biographical plan. The recipient of this letter was one of Paul's companions in whom he placed a considerable amount of trust. It is puzzling that Titus is not mentioned in the Book of Acts among the companions of Paul. Some suggest that this Gentile is not mentioned because he was the brother of Luke, the author of Acts. Out of modesty Luke does not mention himself or his prominent brother.

Chronologically Titus is first mentioned in conjunction with the important Jerusalem conference in AD 50, which dealt with the issue of circumcision. Titus accompanied Paul and Barnabas to Jerusalem (Galatians 2:1). As a Gentile convert Titus provided a test case for the leaders of the church. He put a face on the problem, so to speak. Apparently Titus was not compelled to be circumcised (Galatians 2:3).

Titus probably accompanied Paul on his second and third missionary journeys, but no definite information of his work is available until the time of the Corinthian crisis. Titus evidently had been acting as Paul's representative at Corinth during the year preceding the writing of 2 Corinthians (2 Corinthians 8:16). His mission was to organize the collection for the Jerusalem Christians in the church at Corinth. The task was unfinished, for Titus is later urged by Paul to return to Corinth to see to its completion (2 Corinthians 8:6).

Titus is last mentioned in 2 Timothy 4:10 where Paul had dispatched him to Dalmatia (modern Albania and Slovenia). At the time of the writing of this letter Titus was Paul's representative on the island of Crete. All together Titus is mentioned twelve times in the New Testament.

Four other associates of Paul are mentioned in the Book of Titus. Either *Artemas* (*ahr'-tih-muhs*) or *Tychicus* (3:12) will be sent to relieve Titus in the work on Crete. Nothing is known about the first associate. Tychicus was a native of Asia Minor (Acts 20:4). He traveled with the Apostle Paul on the third missionary journey. Tychicus and Onesimus carried the Colossian letter from Paul (Colossians 4:7-9). Paul also sent Tychicus to Ephesus on one occasion (2 Timothy 4:12).

Zenas and *Apollos* are named as worthy of assistance in their travels when they came to Crete. Nothing is known of Zenas (3:13) except that he was a Christian lawyer. Apollos was a Jew from Alexandria, Egypt. On a visit to Ephesus he was taught Christian doctrine by Priscilla and Aquila (Acts 18:26). Apollos became an articulate and forceful advocate of the Christian faith (Acts 18:28). He was especially skillful in handling the Old Testament prophecies. When Apollos is last mentioned in the Book of Acts, he was in Corinth (Acts 19:1).

Paul referred to Apollos frequently, particularly in 1 Corinthians. Some in Corinth were drawn to Apollos. They tended to segregate themselves from other members of the church (1 Corinthians 1:12; 3:4-6, 22).

Paul respected, even loved, Apollos. He referred to Apollos as *our brother*, showing how much Paul considered him as one of the team (1 Corinthians 16:12). In 1 Corinthians 4:6 Paul placed Apollos on the same level as himself.

Geographical plan. Titus was laboring for the Lord on the island of **Crete** (*kreete*). This island is 156 miles by thirty miles. It lies in the Mediterranean Sea a hundred miles southeast of Greece. In square miles Crete is about the size of the state of Rhode Island. The first century inhabitants of Crete were notorious for untruthfulness and immorality (1:12-13). Some from Crete were present in Jerusalem on the day of Pentecost (Acts 2:11). Perhaps they were the ones who returned to the island to start the Christian work there.

The only other place that is mentioned in Titus is **Nicopolis** (*nih-kahp'-oh-lihs*) (3:12) on the western coast of Greece. Paul intended to spend the winter there. Titus was to meet Paul in Nicopolis when his replacement arrived.

Eternal Purpose

The immediate purpose of the letter to Titus is to offer encouragement and instruction in the ministry of this evangelist among the churches on the island of Crete. The deeper purpose is to stress that sound doctrine and good deeds are essential in the life of every Christian.

Titus contains two outstanding doctrinal passages. In the first Paul speaks of the grace of God that made salvation possible, the doctrine of redemption, the necessity of pure living, and the hope of the Second Coming (2:11-14). In the second Paul speaks of the basis of salvation (grace not works), the washing of rebirth (baptism), and the indwelling presence of the Holy Spirit (3:4-7).

In synopsis, Paul sets forth in Titus precepts for congregational life (ch. 1), family and individual life (ch. 2), and public life (ch. 3).

The basic truth set forth in this book is that we should follow the revealed pattern for the conduct of the church.

Acclaim

The Book of Titus sets forth in very clear terms the deity and redemptive work of Christ (2:13-14). Christ gave himself for us, he redeemed us, purified us, so that we have become his special people. Paul emphasizes the deity of Christ when he refers to him as *our God and Savior* (2:13). The portrait of Jesus that we shall associate with the Book of Titus is **Defender of True Doctrine.**

Keys

The key chapter in Titus is chapter 2. This chapter contains the fundamental commands that must be obeyed if the church is to have godly leadership.

The key verse in the book is this: *The reason I left you in Crete was that you might straighten out what was left unfinished and appoint elders in every town* (1:5).

The key phrase in Titus is *eternal life* (2).

The key words include *speak/exhort* (7) and *grace* (4).

Special Features

Here are some facts that distinguish the Book of Titus in the sacred collection:

- ❖ Some think Titus was the brother of Luke.
- ❖ Paul quotes a heathen poet in 1:12.
- ❖ Titus is not mentioned in the Book of Acts.
- ❖ The maturity of Titus is indicated by the fact that Paul does not exhort him to be strong, or to let no one despise his youth, as he exhorts Timothy.
- ❖ There are about three thousand Orthodox churches on the island of Crete today. Most of the half-million residents of the island consider themselves members of the Orthodox Church of Crete.

HEAR

Some of the favorite passages found in Titus are the following:
- ❖ *To the pure, all things are pure* (1:15).
- ❖ *While we wait for the blessed hope — the glorious appearing of our great God and Savior, Jesus Christ* (2:13).

- *He saved us through the washing of rebirth and renewal by the Holy Spirit* (3:5).
- *One of their own prophets has said, "Cretans are always liars, evil brutes, lazy gluttons* (1:12).

57th Book of the Bible
Book of Philemon
Blessing in Christ

Philemon is the last of the New Testament books generally attributed to Paul. Because Philemon was written from prison at the same time as Ephesians, Philippians, and Colossians, the four epistles are called Paul's *Prison Epistles.*

Philemon is a masterpiece of Christian tact and a model for Christian persuasion. The letter deals with the issue of a slave that had run away from his Christian master. The slave had now become a Christian. Paul does not directly ask Philemon to free the slave. Philemon, however, could not have missed the implications of what Paul was suggesting. Paul applied subtle, but certainly not gentle, persuasion in order to get Philemon to do the right thing.

The letter contains one chapter, twenty-five verses, and 334 words.

Situation

Philemon was a wealthy Christian leader in Colosse. He obviously knew Paul, but in what context is not clear.

Paul had met and converted a runaway slave named Onesimus. Although Onesimus had become a valuable asset to Paul, both Paul and the slave knew that he had a responsibility to return to Colosse, to Philemon his master.

Tychicus carried the three letters (Ephesians, Colossians, Philemon) to the Lycus valley in the Roman province of Asia (in modern Turkey). Onesimus accompanied Tychicus. A date of about AD 63 is appropriate for these three letters.

Plan

Structural plan. The underlying theme of the letter to Philemon is *blessing in Christ*. The emphasis is on the transition from bondage to brotherhood. The letter to Philemon has four distinct divisions. The outline looks like this:

- ❖ **Greeting** (vv. 1-3)
- ❖ **Praise for Philemon** (vv. 4-7)
- ❖ **Petition for Onesimus** (vv. 8-22)
- ❖ **Conclusion** (vv. 23-25)

Biographical plan. The three main parties in the letter to Philemon are **Paul** the writer, who now was in custody in Rome; **Philemon** the recipient, whose slave had run away; and **Onesimus**, the runaway slave who had become a Christian.

In this brief letter Paul mentions six associates, presumably known to Philemon as well. **Timothy** is associated with Paul in the greeting (v. 1). Timothy accompanied Paul on his second and third missionary journeys. He later received two letters from Paul. **Epaphras** is designated as *my fellow-prisoner* (v. 23). He sent greetings to Philemon. Epaphras may have been the founder of the Christian community in Colosse. It was from him that Paul learned of the situation in the church in Colosse (Colossians 1:7). Apparently he was a companion of Paul during the first Roman imprisonment. Paul evidently held this man in high regard.

Four others are named as greeters. This quartet must have been with Paul during his first Roman imprisonment. **Mark** is known for deserting Paul on the first missionary journey. Later he served alongside Peter. He is the author of the second Gospel. **Aristarchus** was the focus of an anti-Christian riot in Ephesus (Acts 19:29). He was the Thessalonian who accompanied Paul from Greece to Jerusalem as he returned from his third missionary journey (Acts 20:4). Aristarchus was with Paul when he as a prisoner sailed for Rome (Acts 27:2). Concerning **Demas** nothing is known except that he was once an honored fellow worker with Paul, but later turned back to the world. **Luke** was the Gentile physician who accompanied Paul on his second and third missionary journeys. Luke was with Paul during his two Roman imprisonments. He was the author of the third Gospel and the Book of Acts.

Two brethren in the church at Colosse are named: **Apphia** (*ap'-fih-uh*) *our sister* and **Archippus** *our fellow soldier.* The former may have been Philemon's wife, the latter his son. For this, however, there is no proof. The language *fellow soldier* suggests that Archippus was a prominent leader—perhaps minister—of the church in Colosse.

Geographical plan. Colosse was about a weeklong trip east of Ephesus, in modern Turkey. On this city see further under Colossians.

Eternal Purpose

The immediate purpose of the letter to Philemon is to induce a wealthy Christian leader to treat a former runaway slave as a brother in the Lord. The deeper purpose of the letter is to teach that brotherhood in Christ transcends all social and economic barriers.

A synopsis of Philemon looks like this: Onesimus the slave was now a brother in Christ. Therefore, Philemon should receive him back as such. Any monetary loss incurred by the slave's running away should be charged to Paul's account.

The basic truth that we should take from this book is this: We should seek to help new members of the Body of Christ as much as possible.

Philemon was not written to teach Christian doctrine, but to apply it. The principles of Christianity when applied correctly have a radical impact on social conditions.

In this letter Paul applies seven "pressure points" to Philemon. Each has an actionable implication. First, Paul compliments Philemon for his love for all God's people (v. 5). By implication, that must include slaves and former slaves. Philemon must extend to Onesimus the same love that he extends to the rest of the saints.

Second, Paul wanted to keep Onesimus with him in Rome. He would not do so, however, without Philemon's permission

(vv. 8-9, 14). The implication is that Paul, as an apostle, had the authority to order Philemon, a church leader, to free Onesimus. Paul chose, however, the way of persuasion.

Third, Paul speaks of Onesimus as his dear friend (v. 12). He asks Philemon to welcome him as a brother. The implication is that Philemon should no more think of punishing Onesimus for running away than he would think of punishing Paul.

Fourth, Paul will make good any losses incurred by Philemon when Onesimus ran away. Philemon, however, must remember that he himself is indebted to Paul (vv. 18-19). The implication is that out of gratitude for what Paul had done for him, Philemon should set Onesimus free.

Fifth, the letter is addressed to the congregation that met in Philemon's home as well as Philemon himself (v. 2). The implication is that others would read the letter and realize what Paul was asking Philemon to do. Fellow Christians might add their peer pressure to get Philemon to free Onesimus.

Sixth, when Paul is released from Roman custody, he plans to visit Philemon (v. 22). The implication is that the reunion with Paul will be awkward if Onesimus is not set free by that time.

Seventh, four associates known to Philemon join Paul in writing this letter (v. 23). The implication is that these associates concur in his request to free Onesimus.

By way of personal application, Philemon presses upon us the responsibility to forgive those who have trespassed against us just as God for Christ's sake has forgiven us. Philemon was shown mercy through the grace of Christ. Now he must graciously forgive his repentant runaway who returns as a brother in Christ.

Acclaim

No one title for Christ "jumps off" the page of Philemon. There is, however, an expression in verse 6 that is fruitful for meditation: *every good thing we have in Christ*. This expression suggests a portrait of Christ as *Repository of all that is Good*. Based on the implications of the entire letter another picture of Christ emerges. Ultimately Christ is **Our Only Master**.

One could also argue that the letter to Philemon illustrates the forgiveness that a believer finds in Christ. By law Onesimus was condemned; he deserved to be punished. Paul appeals for him to be set free (saved) by the grace of his former master even as Philemon had been forgiven by God's grace.

Keys

The key verse in the letter to Philemon is this: *If you consider me a partner, welcome him as you would welcome me* (v. 17).

The key phrase must be: *welcome him as you would welcome me* (v. 17).

Key words include *brother* (4), *our* (4), and *receive* (3).

Special Features

Here are some facts about Philemon that distinguish it in the New Testament collection:

- ❖ Philemon is the shortest of Paul's epistles.
- ❖ Paul lightens up the ugly topic of runaway slaves with a play on words in verse 11. The name *Onesimus* means *useful*. In the past Onesimus had been a troublemaker for Philemon—he was *useless*. Now that he is a Christian, he can live up to his name.
- ❖ Church history records that the leader in the church at Ephesus about fifty years after Paul wrote this letter was named Onesimus. Could this be the same Onesimus?
- ❖ Unlike the other personal letters of Paul (1 & 2 Timothy, Titus) this letter is also addressed to a family and a church (v. 2).
- ❖ Unlike his other epistles, Paul wrote Philemon entirely in his own hand (v. 19).

HEAR

Favorite lines in the letter to Philemon include these:
- ❖ *. . . no longer as a slave, but better than a slave, as a dear brother* (v. 15-16).
- ❖ *Charge it to me* (v. 18).

Section Four

Focus Books

Hebrews
James
1 Peter
2 Peter
1 John
2 John
3 John
Jude

Revelation

Chapter Eleven

Jewish Christian Letters
Hebrews and James

In previous chapters we surveyed the thirteen letters generally acknowledged to have been written by the Apostle Paul. Nine of these letters were written to congregations, and four to individuals. We now come to the fourth shelf of the New Testament library, what we have called the Focus Books or General Epistles.

There are eight epistles on this shelf. These eight can be divided chronologically into two quartets that might be designated the earlier epistles written prior to AD 70 and the later epistles written after that date. The earlier quartet consists of James, Hebrews, 1 & 2 Peter. The later quarter is made up of Jude, 1, 2, & 3 John.

In the eight General Epistles there is a balance of truth that helps Christians keep from veering into extreme positions in respect to Christian teaching. Hebrews stresses faith; but James balances that emphasis by stressing good works. In 1 Peter the apostle has his eye on future hope; but in his second letter he emphasizes present growth. John's epistles stress love; but the epistle of Jude exhorts Christians to contend for the faith once for all delivered to the saints.

58th Book of the Bible
Book of Hebrews
Superiority of Our Faith

In the oldest manuscripts the fifty-eighth book of the Bible is entitled *Hebrews*. The epistle makes no claim of authorship. The writer, however, was known to the original readers (13:18-24).

The strongest tradition is that Paul wrote this letter to Hebrew Christians. There are certain differences in writing style between Paul's letters and this book. Writing style, however, differs according to the circumstance of writing and the subject matter being addressed. The language of 2:3 suggests that the writer was not one of the original Twelve. Paul remains a viable candidate for the authorship of this book. Others have proposed that Barnabas or Apollos wrote Hebrews.

We call the Book of Hebrews an epistle. It actually reads more like a sermonic essay than a letter. It contains a brilliant argument for the superiority of the Christian faith over Judaism. The writer employs a scholarly and precise style of writing. For literary quality Hebrews is unexcelled in the New Testament. The book was written for Jewish Christians who were contemplating giving up their new faith and returning to Judaism.

The Book of Hebrews contains thirteen chapters, 303 verses, and 6,913 words. It is over twice the size of the next longest of the General Epistles.

Situation

Because of persecution, isolation, and/or family pressure, many Jewish Christians were slipping back into Judaism, a legal religion in the Roman Empire. The book appears to anticipate the Roman destruction of Jerusalem. Thus it was written prior to AD 70. Beyond this there is nothing that can be said about where or when Hebrews was written. Likewise no agreement exists about the location of the original readers. The majority opinion is that the book was written to Jewish Christians in Rome. There is no good reason, however, to abandon the traditional view that *To the*

Hebrews means the Hebrew people living in Jerusalem. The book was written about AD 64. It may have been written while Paul was under house arrest in Rome, or shortly after his release. The language of 13:24 is grounds for the traditional view that the book was written from Italy (Rome).

Plan

Structural plan. The theme of this book is the *superiority of Christ*. The Book of Hebrews has three main divisions that are followed by a conclusion. The outline of the book looks like this:

- ❖ **Christ Is Superior in His Word** (1:1–4:13)
- ❖ **Christ Is Superior in His Work** (4:14–10:18)
- ❖ **Christ Is Superior in His Way** (10:19–13:17)
- ❖ **Conclusion** (13:18-25)

The first division proves that Christ is superior in his word to prophets of the Old Testament, to angels, or even to Moses. The second division makes the point that the work of Christ is superior to that of the Old Testament priesthood, covenant, and sacrificial system. The third division drives home the point that the way of Christ—the way of faith and love—is superior to anything that preceded it.

Biographical plan. Only one well-known Christian leader is mentioned in Hebrews. ***Timothy*** recently had been *set free*. The writer appears to have been waiting somewhere for Timothy to join him. He intended to travel to the area where the letter's recipients resided in the company of Timothy.

Twenty-two Old Testament characters are mentioned by name in Hebrews. From the earliest chapters of Genesis the writer mentions *Abel* (11:4; 12:24) and his brother *Cain* (11:4), *Enoch* (11:5), and *Noah* (11:7).

From the Pilgrim Period Hebrews names *Abraham* (13×) and his wife *Sarah* (11:11), *Isaac* (5×), *Jacob* (3×) and his brother *Esau* (11:20; 12:16), *Joseph* (11:20), *Melchizedek* (8×), and *Levi* (4×).

From the Egyptian and Wilderness periods Hebrews names *Moses* (11×), *Aaron* (5:4; 7:11), and *Pharaoh's daughter* (11:24).

From the Conquest and Judges periods Hebrews names *Rahab* (11:31), *Gideon* (11:32), *Barak* (11:32), *Samson* (11:32), *Jephthah* (11:32), and *Samuel* (11:32)

From the Single Kingdom Period Hebrews names *David* (4:7; 11:32).

Geographical plan. Hebrews mentions one country that was contemporary with the writing of the letter. He sends to the recipients greetings from those in *Italy* (13:24). From Old Testament history the writer mentions *Jerusalem* (12:22). He also makes mention of *Salem* (7:1, 2), the pre-Israelite name for Jerusalem as well as the name *Mount Zion* (12:22) by which the place was frequently referred to by the prophets. He alludes to *Egypt,* the *Red Sea,* and *Jericho* as places where the power of faith was demonstrated (11:26, 29, 30).

Eternal Purpose

The immediate purpose of the Book of Hebrews is to convince wavering Jewish Christians that Jesus fulfilled God's promises to Israel, and that the new covenant is far superior to the old. The deeper purpose of the book is to set forth teaching regarding the heavenly ministry of Jesus Christ and to urge believers to become mature in the Lord.

A synopsis of the Book of Hebrews looks like this: Christ is worthy of our faith. He is better than angels, Moses, Joshua, and Aaron. Therefore, Christians should have faith in Christ and not fall away.

We should take from this book the fundamental truth that we must hang on to Jesus if we want to enjoy our salvation forever.

Hebrews is a theological heavyweight among the New Testament books. The book is especially rich in its revelation of the present priestly ministry of Christ on behalf of the believer. It develops the doctrine of the atoning work of Christ in relation to the New Covenant. Here also one can find a discussion of the typological (prophetic) significance of the offerings and feasts of the Old Testament. A Christian understanding of the Old Testament is virtually impossible without this book.

Some of the strongest teachings in the Bible on the consequences of apostasy—totally abandoning the Christian faith—are found in Hebrews (6:1-4; 10:26-29). There is a point of no return in the downward spiral of rejection of God by those who once embraced Christian truth. The teaching of this book is devastating to those who teach that the truly saved can never lose their salvation.

Acclaim

The lasting portrait of Christ painted by the writer of Hebrews is that Jesus is the **Perfect Savior,** or to use the language of the writer himself, *the author and perfecter of our faith* (12:2). Jesus is the perfect Savior because he presented before God the perfect sacrifice for sin—his own blood. Because his sacrifice was perfect, it did not need to be offered repeatedly, as did the Old Testament sacrifices. Because he was sinless (4:15), he could save us.

Jesus is not only the perfect sacrifice, he is the perfect high priest. By coming in the flesh Christ identified with us. He is able to sympathize with our weaknesses (4:15). His resurrection and ascension enabled him to enter directly into the presence of God. He sits now at the right hand of the Father where he has direct access and influence on our behalf (1:3; 10:12). Christ combines in his own person the offices of priest and king, like the ancient Melchizedek the priest-king of Salem (Jerusalem).

Hebrews also makes the point that Jesus was the perfect Prophet. He communicated God's word better and more authoritatively than any angel or prophet, or even Moses himself. His is the final word from heaven by which all other revelations are measured. The deity of Christ (1:1-3, 8) and his humanity (2:9, 14, 17-18) are both powerfully affirmed in this book. Over twenty titles are used to describe Christ's attributes and accomplishments. In him God's plan for the ages culminates.

Three great appearances of Christ are stressed in Hebrews. In the past Christ lived on the earth and died on the cross as the perfect sacrifice (9:26). Presently Christ is seated in heaven as our High Priest at the right hand of the throne (9:24). In the future Christ will appear in the clouds of glory (9:28) as our victorious King.

Keys

The key chapter in the Book of Hebrews is chapter 11. This is called *the great faith chapter*. It lists those in Old Testament history who willingly and courageously took God at his word.

The key verse in the book is this: *We must pay more careful attention, therefore, to what we have heard, so that we do not drift away* (Hebrews 2:1).

Key words include *perfect* (14), *eternal, forever* (15), *better* (13), *partakers* (9), *heaven* (17), and *priest, high priest* (32).

Special Features

Here are some of the unique features of Hebrews that distinguish it among the books of the New Testament.

- ❖ Hebrews has been called the fifth Gospel, for it tells what Christ is now doing in heaven.
- ❖ Romans reveals the necessity of the Christian faith; Hebrews reveals its superiority.
- ❖ There are eighty-six direct references to the Old Testament taken from ten passages.
- ❖ Hebrews makes exclusive use of the Septuagint (Greek translation) of the Old Testament. One might properly conclude that this was the favorite translation of the original recipients of this epistle.
- ❖ Hebrews is the only New Testament book whose authorship remains a real mystery.

HEAR

Some of the favorite lines from Hebrews might whet your appetite for digging into this wonderful book.

- ❖ *In the past God spoke to our forefathers through the prophets at many times and in various ways, but in these last days he has spoken to us by his Son* (1:1-2).
- ❖ *See to it, brothers, that none of you has a sinful, unbelieving heart that turns away from the living God* (3:12).

- ❖ *For the word of God is living and active. Sharper than any double-edged sword, it penetrates even to dividing soul and spirit, joints and marrow . . .* (4:12).
- ❖ *We do not have a high priest who is unable to sympathize with our weaknesses, but we have one who has been tempted in every way, just as we are—yet was without sin* (4:15).
- ❖ *It is impossible for those who have been enlightened, who have tasted the heavenly gift, who have shared in the Holy Spirit, who have tasted the goodness of the word of God and the powers of the coming age, if they fall away, to be brought back to repentance, because to their loss they are crucifying the Son of God all over again and subjecting him to public disgrace* (6:4-6).
- ❖ *If we deliberately keep on sinning after we have received the knowledge of the truth, no sacrifice for sins is left* (10:26).
- ❖ *Let us run with perseverance the race marked out for us* (12:1).
- ❖ *But you have come to Mount Zion, to the heavenly Jerusalem, the city of the living God* (12:22).
- ❖ *Marriage should be honored by all, and the marriage bed kept pure* (13:4).
- ❖ *Jesus Christ is the same yesterday and today and forever* (13:8).

59th Book of the Bible
Book of James
Application of Our Faith

The author of this book is not the Apostle James who was beheaded in Acts 12. This writer is James the oldest half brother of Jesus (Mark 6:3; Matthew 13:55).

The beloved Book of James is all about walking the walk—living up to the principles of our Christian faith. For this writer Christianity is not just a matter of holding to a correct set of beliefs. Orthodoxy without daily obedience is cold and sterile. Only a faith that transforms our behavior is truly Christian. James presents a series of concrete situations. He leads his readers to realize their Christian responsibility in each of those situations.

James is the most practical book in the New Testament. It is as relevant today as it was when it was written. The exhortations of James concerning trials and temptations, response to God's word, favoritism, control of the tongue, and the lure of worldliness are strongly needed in the contemporary church.

The Book of James contains five chapters, 108 verses, and 2,309 words.

Situation

When James wrote this epistle, the membership of the church was largely Jewish. The Jewish Christians for whom he wrote needed to put their faith into practice. A date of about AD 48 is appropriate for this book. This was about the time when Paul was beginning to make his missionary journeys to establish largely Gentile churches throughout Asia Minor and Greece.

Plan

James writes with a very clear and concise style. His tone is authoritative. The book reads like an odd mix of Solomon in Proverbs and Amos in one of his impassioned appeals. James does not mince words when it comes to exposing hypocritical or unethical conduct. He writes in a good quality Greek. He uses vivid imagery, especially from nature, to communicate his thoughts. Unlike Paul, James says nothing about his personal circumstances.

Structural plan. *Demonstration of the Faith* is the theme of the Epistle of James. Each chapter of the book focuses on a different way in which the Christian can prove to the world the reality of his faith. The outline looks like this:

- ❖ **Confront Trials Cheerfully** (ch. 1)
- ❖ **Consider All Men Equally** (ch. 2)
- ❖ **Control the Tongue Totally** (ch. 3)
- ❖ **Cleanse the Mind Completely** (ch. 4)
- ❖ **Cry Out to God Fervently** (ch. 5)

Biographical plan. The writer of James is a fascinating example of the transforming power of the resurrection of Jesus. Prior to the resurrection James was an unbeliever (John 7:3-10). The triumphant Christ, however, appeared to him (1 Corinthians 15:7). His life was changed forever. James was among the 120 closest disciples of Jesus who waited in the upper room for Pentecost (Acts 1:14).

Paul met James on his first trip to Jerusalem (Galatians 1:18, 19). James spoke at the Jerusalem conference in support of Paul's work. He also conferred with Paul during the apostle's last trip to Jerusalem.

Paul alludes to James in 1 Corinthians 9:5 as one of the leaders of the church. In the early church he was surnamed, "the Just" on account of his piety. Church history says he spent so much time in prayer that his knees became hard and calloused like a camel's knees. James died by being thrown from the pinnacle of the temple for refusing to reject Christ before the Sanhedrin. As he lay dying from the fall he was stoned to death.

James mentions four Old Testament characters. He speaks of *Abraham*, who was justified by his works (2:21). Abraham demonstrated his faith by offering up *Isaac* on the altar, howbeit spiritually speaking (2:21). *Rahab* the harlot was also justified by her works (2:25). James speaks of *Elijah* the prophet, who prayed that it might not rain (5:17).

Geographical plan. No specific locations are mentioned in this epistle. James addresses his writing to *the twelve tribes which are scattered abroad* (1:1). He means either 1) Jewish Christians living outside of Palestine (1:19; 2:1, 7); or 2) the entire Christian church which James is portraying as the New Israel.

Eternal Purpose

The immediate purpose of the Epistle of James is to encourage Christians who were facing problems that were testing their faith. The deeper purpose of the book is to set forth the characteristics of true faith.

A synopsis of this book looks like this: faith is tested by trials (ch. 1), proven through works (ch. 2), demonstrated by conduct (ch. 3), and experienced through persecution (ch. 4-5).

From this book we learn the lesson that we must demonstrate our faith in good works (2:26).

James has little formal theology. Yet there are a few doctrinal statements in the book (1:12-13, 17-18; 2:1, 10-13, 19; 3:9; 4:5; 5:7-9).

The great teaching of the book is that true faith must work; it must produce; it must be visible. Faith that never gets beyond mind or mouth is not sufficient. Certainly faith must be there, but it must be more. The noun *faith* must be translated into an action verb.

How does faith behave? It endures trials, defeats temptations, and obeys divine commands. Faith rejects prejudice, displays itself in practical good deeds, and controls the tongue. It acts wisely, results in separation from the world, and resists the devil. Faith draws near to God and waits patiently for the Lord. Such is Christian faith as James knows it.

Acclaim

James is saturated with allusions to the teachings of Christ. The Sermon on the Mount was especially prominent in his thinking. There are fifteen indirect references to it. Compared to other New Testament writers, however, James says little about the person of Jesus. He refers to him twice as *the Lord Jesus Christ* (1:1; 2:1). He also refers to *the coming of the Lord* (5:7-8). The portrait of Jesus that we will associate with James is the **Judge *[at the Door]*** (5:9).

Keys

The key chapter in the Book of James is chapter 1. This chapter reveals the Christian's proper response to trials and testing.

The key verse in the book is this: *As the body without the spirit is dead, so faith without deeds is dead* (2:26).

The key phrase is *[my] brethren* (11) or *my beloved brethren* (3).

Key words include *faith* (14) and *works* (13).

For those who pit James with his emphasis on works against Paul with his emphasis on faith, it comes as a shock to discover that the word *faith* is found more often in James than in Galatians. It has well been said that faith alone saves, but the faith that saves is not alone! Another way of putting it is that Paul focused on the root of salvation, James upon its fruit.

Special Features

Some outstanding features of this book are these:

- ❖ Many think that James is the earliest book of the New Testament.
- ❖ James is said to be the most Jewish book in the New Testament.
- ❖ James is the interpretation of the Old Testament Law and the Sermon on the Mount in the light of the gospel.
- ❖ The Greek language of James is of the highest quality.
- ❖ Only four direct quotes from the Old Testament are found in James, but at least fifty-three Old Testament allusions.
- ❖ Martin Luther regarded James as "an epistle of straw" because he perceived that James contradicted Paul on the issue of salvation by faith (see James 2:24 and Ephesians 2:8, 9).
- ❖ James has been called "the Proverbs of the New Testament" because it is written in the terse moralistic style of the Old Testament wisdom literature. The contrast between human and divine wisdom in 3:15-17 is reminiscent of the Book of Proverbs.
- ❖ James's impassioned preaching against inequity and social injustice has earned him the title "the Amos of the New Testament."
- ❖ James is a formal, impersonal, and sometimes severe epistle. It rings with authority, averaging one imperative every other verse.
- ❖ James alludes to nature more than any other New Testament book.

HEAR

Here are some favorite lines to whet your appetite for a deeper study of the Epistle of James:

- ❖ *Consider it pure joy, my brothers, whenever you face trials of many kinds* (1:2).

- *If any of you lacks wisdom, he should ask God (1:5).*
- *When tempted, no one should say, "God is tempting me." For God cannot be tempted by evil, nor does he tempt anyone (1:13).*
- *No man can tame the tongue (3:8).*
- *Resist the devil, and he will flee from you (4:7).*
- *What is your life? You are a mist that appears for a little while and then vanishes (4:14).*
- *The prayer offered in faith will make the sick person well; the Lord will raise him up (5:15).*
- *Everyone should be quick to listen, slow to speak and slow to become angry (1:19).*

Chapter Twelve

Letters from an Apostle and a Brother
1 & 2 Peter, Jude

The two letters written by Peter are called by biblical scholars the Petrine epistles. Because of similarity of content, the little epistle of Jude is usually discussed along with 2 Peter. For this reason we will consider Jude in this lesson out of biblical order.

60th Book of the Bible
Book of 1 Peter
Suffering for Our Faith

As the name implies, this is the first of two New Testament epistles written by the Big Fisherman, Simon Peter. Based upon the content of his first epistle, Peter has been called *the Apostle of Hope* (1 Peter 1:3, 13, 21; 3:15).

The first epistle of Peter contains five chapters, 105 verses, and 2,482 words.

Situation

Not much can be said about the circumstances that led Peter to pen his first epistle. The content indicates that Peter was writing in the midst of a terrible persecution. Most likely this was the persecution of Christians by the Emperor Nero. A date of about AD 65 is generally accepted as the time of writing. This was the same time frame as the writing of 2 Timothy. The destruction of Jerusalem by the Romans was yet five years in the future.

Plan

Some see evidences of the influence of Paul in the style and content of 1 Peter. This is not surprising since Peter wrote with the help of Silas (5:12), one of Paul's closest associates. Be that as it may, Peter in this epistle displays genuine warmth and sympathy for the plight of his readers. On the other hand, Peter deals with various issues forcefully. There is a chain of thirty-four imperatives from 1:13 to 5:9. Yet these authoritative pronouncements are tempered by the apostle's compassion.

In his inaugural sermon in Acts 2 Peter displayed a marvelous command of Old Testament facts and insight into the meaning of prophecies. The same is true of this epistle. Peter also makes reference to a number of his personal experiences with Christ.

Structural plan. The theme of 1 Peter is *suffering for the faith.* The epistle has three major divisions sandwiched between a brief introduction and conclusion. The outline of 1 Peter looks like this:

- ❖ **Introduction** (1:1-2)
- ❖ **Salvation of the Believer** (1:3–2:12)
- ❖ **Submission of the Believer** (2:13–3:12)
- ❖ **Suffering of the Believer** (3:13–5:9)
- ❖ **Conclusion** (5:10-14)

The emphasis in the first major division is on assurance. In the second division it is holiness that is stressed. The third division emphasizes victory.

Biographical plan. The writer of this epistle is one of the prominent leaders in the early church. Peter's name appears 176 times in the New Testament. This compares to 202 appearances of Paul's name and the rest of the apostles a combined 142 times.

During the ministry of Jesus, Peter was the spokesman for the Twelve. He was one of the "inner circle" that was permitted to be with Jesus on very special occasions. In a moment of weakness on the night of Jesus' arrest Peter cursed and denied three times that he even knew his Master. After his resurrection, Jesus forgave Peter and reinstated him in his position of apostle (John 21:15-17).

The first half of the Book of Acts focuses on the ministry of Peter in the life of the early church. Several spectacular miracles are attributed to him, including the resurrection of Dorcas from the dead. References to Peter in the epistles indicate that he labored at Antioch (Galatians 2:11ff.), Corinth (1 Corinthians 1:12), Asia Minor (1 Peter 1:1), and "Babylon," a Christian code name for Rome (1 Peter 5:13).

According to early Christian tradition Peter died in Rome. He requested to be crucified upside down because he did not feel worthy to die in the same manner as his Savior.

Two of Peter's associates are named in the epistle. **Silvanus** or *Silas* assisted in penning the letter, probably as Peter's scribe. According to the Book of Acts Silas accompanied Paul on his second and third missionary journeys. Peter refers to **Mark** as *my son*. Mark was associated with Paul on the first missionary journey. Later he teamed up with Barnabas his cousin. During his first Roman imprisonment Paul referred to Mark as a *fellow laborer* (Philemon 24).

Peter mentions three Old Testament characters. He alludes to the days of **Noah**, the ark, and the deliverance of Noah's family from the Flood (3:20). Peter mentions the respect that **Sarah** showed toward her husband **Abraham** (3:6).

Geographical plan. Peter indicates that he was writing from "Babylon." Early tradition indicates that this was a code designation for Rome. For comments on the city of Rome at this time see under Romans.

The addressees of this epistle were living in five Roman provinces located in what we call today Turkey. **Pontus** is mentioned three times. Paul's friend Aquila came from Pontus (Acts 18:2). There were some from Pontus present on the day of Pentecost in Jerusalem (Acts 2:9). **Galatia** is mentioned five times in the New Testament. Paul evangelized in this area on his missionary journeys. He also wrote a letter to the churches of Galatia. There were some present in Jerusalem on Pentecost from *Cappadocia* (*kap-puh-doh'-see-uh*) (Acts 2:9). Nothing is known of how Christian work started in this area. The Roman province of *Asia* is mentioned nineteen times in the New Testament. Paul was forbidden by the Spirit to preach in Asia on his second journey (Acts 16:6), but returned there on his third journey for an extended stay (Acts 19). Paul was prevented by the Spirit from preaching in *Bithynia* (*bih-thihn'-ih-uh*) on his second missionary journey. Peter may have pioneered the work in this area.

Eternal Purpose

The immediate purpose of Peter's first epistle is to encourage the believers in "Turkey" who were facing growing opposition. The deeper purpose is to set forth for all believers the proper response to suffering.

A synopsis of the book looks like this: Christians should walk in harmony with the living hope that we profess. Christ is the example for our holy conduct. All areas of life should reflect the hope that is within us.

From this epistle we should take the basic truth that we must suffer patiently to the glory of God.

This epistle makes a significant contribution to the teaching of the New Testament; but the teachings are not systematically developed. Peter has important things to say about the doctrine of salvation (1:2, 15, 23); the doctrine of the church (2:5, 9-10; 5:2); and eschatology, the doctrine of final things (1:7, 13; 4:7, 13; 5:4).

Acclaim

In respect to the doctrine of Christ, 1 Peter is rich. Peter emphasizes Christ's nature (1:15, 17; 2:22; 4:5, 19), his work (1:18; 2:24; 3:18, 21), and his sufferings (1:11). This epistle presents Christ as the believer's hope in times of suffering (1:3-4). Our relationship with him by faith is a source of inexpressible joy (1:8). His suffering and death provide redemption for all who trust in him (2:24). Christ is our Shepherd and Guardian (2:25; 5:4). When he returns, those who know him will be glorified (1:7).

There are several striking pictures of Christ including *the Living Stone and Precious Cornerstone* (2:4) and the *Shepherd and Guardian of the Soul* (2:25). The Christ portrait that we will associate with 1 Peter is that of the ***Perfect Example*** (2:21).

Keys

The key chapter in 1 Peter is chapter 4. This is the key text of all Scripture on how to handle persecution for one's faith.

The key verse is this: *If you suffer as a Christian, do not be ashamed, but praise God that you bear that name* (1 Peter 4:16).

Key words include *holy* (8), *suffered/suffering* (7), and *faith* (5).

Special Features

Here are some facts about 1 Peter that distinguish it among the books of Scripture:

- ❖ Peter uses a code name for the place of his writing—*Babylon* (5:13).
- ❖ More titles for believers are found in 1 Peter than any other New Testament book.
- ❖ More than a hundred parallels in teaching and wording between Ephesians and 1 Peter have been noted.
- ❖ There are seven different Greek words translated *suffering* in 1 Peter. The theme of suffering is mentioned sixteen times, at least five of which refer to the suffering of Christ on the cross.
- ❖ Peter's first letter can be compared to the Book of Job in the Old Testament because it stresses fidelity to God in the midst of unbearable suffering.
- ❖ Peter credits Silvanus (Silas) with helping to write this letter (5:12). He may have been responsible for the polished Greek of the epistle.

HEAR

Some of the favorite lines in 1 Peter are the following:
- ❖ *Praise be to the God and Father of our Lord Jesus Christ! In his great mercy he has given us new birth into a living hope through the resurrection of Jesus Christ from the dead* (1:3).

- *You know that it was not with perishable things such as silver and gold that you were redeemed from the empty way of life handed down to you from your forefathers, but with the precious blood of Christ, a lamb without blemish or defect (1:18-19)*
- *Like newborn babies, crave pure spiritual milk, so that by it you may grow up in your salvation (2:2).*
- *You also, like living stones, are being built into a spiritual house to be a holy priesthood, offering spiritual sacrifices acceptable to God through Jesus Christ (2:5).*
- *Submit yourselves for the Lord's sake to every authority instituted among men (2:13).*
- *Do not repay evil with evil (3:9).*
- *This water symbolizes baptism that now saves you also – not the removal of dirt from the body but the pledge of a good conscience toward God. It saves you by the resurrection of Jesus Christ (3:21).*
- *Above all, love each other deeply, because love covers over a multitude of sins (4:8).*
- *Cast all your anxiety on him because he cares for you (5:7).*
- *Your enemy the devil prowls around like a roaring lion looking for someone to devour (5:8).*

61st Book of the Bible
Book of 2 Peter
Growing in Our Faith

In his first epistle Peter dealt with problems that arise for Christians from outside the church. In this second letter Peter deals with problems that arise within the church. In 1 Peter the apostle urged submission as the proper response to suffering from without; in 2 Peter he stresses knowledge of the truth as the only preventative to error from within the church.

Peter's second epistle has many similarities with the Epistle of Jude. This epistle also has been compared to 2 Timothy, Paul's last letter. Both contain a key passage on inspiration (2 Peter 1:20;

1 & 2 Peter, Jude

2 Timothy 3:16). Both warn against false teachers. In both the writer anticipates a martyr's death.

The brief letter that we call 2 Peter was not mentioned by the earliest church fathers. Not until the days of the Christian scholar Origen (about AD 225) was it identified as coming from Peter. Early Greek papyrus manuscripts of the New Testament, however, show this epistle was definitely accepted by the church as part of the Christian Scriptures.

The second epistle of Peter contains three chapters, sixty-one verses, and 1,559 words.

Situation

Not much can be said about the circumstances that produced 2 Peter. It is clear that the writer was about to depart this life, probably during the persecution by the Emperor Nero. A date of about AD 67 is appropriate for this epistle. This is the same time frame as the writing of Paul's last letter, 2 Timothy. The destruction of Jerusalem was about three years in the future.

Plan

Structural plan. The theme of 2 Peter is *growing in the faith*. The three chapters reflect three different tones. Chapter 1 is an exhortation, chapter 2 is a warning, and chapter 3 is a defense. In terms of content, the outline looks like this:

- ❖ **Introduction** (1:1-2)
- ❖ **Grow in Christ** (1:3-21)
- ❖ **Beware of Corrupters** (ch. 2)
- ❖ **Hope in the Second Coming** (ch. 3)

Biographical plan. For the highlights of the writer's life, see under 1 Peter. In this epistle Peter's death was imminent. **Paul** is mentioned. In one of the greatest understatements of all time, Peter says that some things that Paul wrote are hard to understand (3:16).

Three Old Testament characters are mentioned: **Noah** is described as *a preacher of righteousness* (2:5). **Lot** is said to have been *greatly distressed by the filthy lives* of those who lived in Sodom (2:7). **Balaam** *son of Beor* who sold out the people of God is said to have *loved the wages of wickedness* (2:15).

Geographical plan. Neither the place of writing (probably Rome) nor the destination of 2 Peter is known. Peter mentions two notorious Old Testament cities. The destruction of ***Sodom*** and ***Gomorrah*** is cited as an example to those who choose to live ungodly.

Eternal Purpose

The immediate purpose of the second epistle of Peter is to combat the rise of heretical teaching within the body of believers. The deeper purpose of this book is to set forth the contrast between the knowledge and practice of the truth versus falsehood.

In synopsis format 2 Peter is an exhortation to grow in the knowledge of Christ and a warning to beware of false prophets.

Christians should take from this book the basic truth that we must grow in the grace of God.

The writer of Hebrews sets forth the antidote to pressure to revert to Judaism as hanging on to Jesus. The message of this book is similar. Peter's exhortation to Christians confronted by new and strange teachings is this: don't give up the faith.

Acclaim

The second epistle of Peter stresses that Jesus is Lord. He is the source of full knowledge and power for reaching spiritual maturity (1:2-3, 8; 3:18). Peter recalls the glory of the transfiguration of Jesus (1:17-18). He anticipates Christ's return in glory. The lasting portrait of Jesus that 2 Peter sketches is the ***Beloved Son*** (1:17).

Keys

The key chapter in 2 Peter is chapter 1. This chapter contains the clearest passage in the Bible defining the relationship between God and man in the process of inspiration.

The key verse in this book is this: *Grow in the grace and knowledge of our Lord and Savior Jesus Christ* (3:18).

The key phrase is the combination of *Lord* with the words *Savior* and/or *Jesus Christ* (8).

The key word is *knowledge* and equivalent words (16).

Special Features

As with each of the books of the Bible, there are certain features that are distinctive of 2 Peter.

- ❖ The early church was at first reluctant to accept this epistle as genuine because of supposed differences in style and vocabulary with 1 Peter.
- ❖ 2 Peter furnishes the only interconnective reference from one apostolic epistle to another when Peter refers to Paul's writings (3:15-16).
- ❖ This epistle confirms that the story of Balaam's talking donkey (Numbers 22:30) should be interpreted as historical, not as a parable (2:16).
- ❖ This epistle contains the only eyewitness description of the transfiguration of Jesus (1:16-18).

HEAR

Here are some favorite lines from Peter's second epistle:

- ❖ *Add to your faith goodness; and to goodness, knowledge; and to knowledge, self-control; and to self-control, perseverance; and to perseverance, godliness; and to godliness, brotherly kindness; and to brotherly kindness, love* (1:5-7).
- ❖ *I think it is right to refresh your memory as long as I live in the tent of this body, because I know that shortly I will soon put it aside, as our Lord Jesus Christ has made clear to me* (1:13-14).
- ❖ *No prophecy of Scripture came about by the prophet's own interpretation. For prophecy never had its origin in the will of man, but men spoke from God as they were carried along by the Holy Spirit* (1:20-21).
- ❖ *If they have escaped the corruption of the world by knowing our Lord and Savior Jesus Christ and are again entangled in*

it and overcome, they are worse off at the end than they were at the beginning. It would have been better for them not to have known the way of righteousness, than to have known it and then to turn their backs on the sacred command that was passed on to them. Of them the proverbs are true: "A dog returns to its vomit," and, "a sow that is washed goes back to her wallowing in the mud" (2:20-22).

❖ *The day of the Lord will come like a thief. The heavens will disappear with a roar; the elements will be destroyed by fire, and the earth and everything in it will be laid bare. . . . But in keeping with his promise we are looking forward to a new heaven and a new earth, the home of righteousness* (3:10-13).

❖ *With the Lord a day is like a thousand years, and a thousand years are like a day* (3:8).

65th Book of the Bible
Book of Jude
Battle for Our Faith

There are eight men named Judas or Jude in the New Testament. The writer of this letter was the brother of James and Jesus (Mark 6:3).

Jude started out to write a positive treatise on salvation. Recent reports about the inroads of false doctrine into the body of Christ compelled him to change directions. Jude took up his pen and produced the New Testament's strongest condemnation of false teachers and teachings.

The message of Jude bears some striking similarities to the writing of his brother James. Like James, Jude used highly descriptive and stinging words to describe those who compromise the truth. Both brothers are fond of nature imagery. Both use a very succinct style of writing. Both stress ethical purity. Both display deep love for their readers in spite of their stern approach. Though James and Jude were raised in the same household with Jesus, in opening words each refers to himself as Jesus' *servant* (lit., *slave*).

Jude contains one chapter, twenty-five verses, and 613 words.

Situation

Persecution temporarily had died down in the Roman Empire under the reign of the Emperor Vespasian. Ungodly men, however, had infiltrated the church, denying the Lord Jesus Christ (v. 4). Their behavior was of the worst sort in that they professed to be Christians and participated in the ordinances (v. 17), but were devoid of spiritual life (v. 19). A date of about AD 75 is appropriate for Jude.

Plan

Structural plan. Jude is so short it is more like a postcard than an epistle. The theme of Jude is *contending for the faith*. The epistle has two main but unequal divisions. The outline looks like this:

- ❖ **Introduction** (1-4)
- ❖ **Warnings about False Teachers** (5-19)
- ❖ **Exhortations to Faithful Believers** (20-23)
- ❖ **Conclusion** (24-25).

Biographical plan. Jude identifies himself as *a servant of Jesus Christ and brother of James.* There is only one James who could be identified without further stipulation and that is James the half brother of Jesus and writer of the epistle that bears his name. Like Jesus' other relatives, initially Jude did not believe (John 7:3-8). He must have become a convert during the forty days of appearances after Jesus' resurrection. Perhaps it was the one-on-one appearance to James that convinced Jude of the reality of the resurrection. In any case, Jude was present with the apostles and other believers in the upper room after the ascension (Acts 1:13). Apparently Jude was married and was accompanied by his wife in missionary endeavors (1 Corinthians 9:5).

Jude mentions **Michael** the archangel who contended with the devil over the body of **Moses** (v. 9). The issue was probably one of averting the danger of the Israelites making a mummified icon out of the corpse of the great leader.

Jude mentions a trio of Old Testament evildoers. He speaks about the way of **Cain,** the error of **Balaam,** and the rebellion of

Korah (v. 11). Cain had an envious and murderous spirit. Because of greed Balaam made a filthy suggestion that could have destroyed the holiness of God's people. Korah led a rebellion against the authority of Moses and Aaron.

Jude also mentions ***Enoch*** the seventh from ***Adam*** who prophesied the coming of the Lord in judgment (v. 14).

Geographical plan. Jude does not identify specifically those for whom he is writing. What he has to say is appropriate for the church anywhere in any period of Christian history.

From the Old Testament Jude speaks of the land of ***Egypt*** from which God saved his people (v. 5). He references the destruction of the cities of ***Sodom*** and ***Gomorrah*** as a warning of the judgment of eternal fire.

Eternal Purpose

The immediate purpose of the epistle of Jude is to expose and condemn the apostasy in the church. The deeper purpose of the book is to urge believers to contend for the truth.

A synopsis of the book looks like this: Christians must contend for the faith remembering that God has judged the wicked in the past, and he will do so again in the future.

Christians should take from this book the basic truth that we must be on guard against those who pervert our Christian faith.

Jude minces no words when he describes the consequences of disobedience to the Lord. He references the severity of the Lord respecting those Israelites who did not believe, the angels who left their proper habitation, and the cities of Sodom and Gomorrah that went after strange flesh.

Acclaim

Jude presents Christ as the one who preserves believers in the midst of persecution from without and corruption from within (v. 1). It is through Jesus Christ that God keeps believers from stumbling and presents them faultless in the final day (v. 24). Jude teaches his readers to *wait for the mercy* of Christ to be revealed at his coming (v. 21). The portrait of Jesus that we will associate with the epistle of Jude, however, is ***Our Only Master*** (v. 4).

1 & 2 Peter, Jude

Keys

The key verse in the epistle of Jude is this: *Contend for the faith that was once for all entrusted to the saints* (v. 3).

Key words include *ungodly* (3) and *beloved* (3).

Special Features

Some of the distinguishing characteristics of the epistle of Jude are these:

- ❖ Because this book chronicles the activities of false teachers, some have referred to this letter as the Acts of the Apostates.
- ❖ Jude is the only book in the Bible devoted entirely to the subject of apostasy.
- ❖ Jude is very similar to 2 Peter. Peter saw the false teachers in the future; in Jude they are already at work. Of twenty-five verses in Jude, nineteen are repeated from 2 Peter.
- ❖ Some think Jude refers to two noncanonical books—the Assumption of Moses (v. 9) and the Book of Enoch (vv. 14, 15).
- ❖ Jude shows a preference for symmetrical balance. He uses groups of three frequently. See verses 1, 2, 5-7, 11, 24-25.

HEAR

God has spoken through Jude, and we need to hear what he says. Two verses from Jude are commonly quoted as a benediction concluding a Christian assembly:

- ❖ *To him who is able to keep you from falling and to present you before his glorious presence without fault and with great joy—to the only God our Savior be glory, majesty, power and authority, through Jesus Christ our Lord, before all ages, now and forevermore! Amen* (vv. 24-25).

Chapter Thirteen

A Letter and Two Postcards

1, 2, & 3 John

Three letters are attributed to the Apostle John in ancient manuscripts and Christian tradition. The first is truly a letter. Because of their size, the other two are more like notes or postcards. John does not mention his name in these three writings. Because of his age he refers to himself as *the elder* in two of them.

All three of John's epistles develop the theme of fellowship: fellowship with God (1 John), fellowship with false teachers (2 John), and fellowship with Christian evangelists (3 John). The importance of these three epistles can hardly be overstated. Perhaps there is no better place in the New Testament to go to remind ourselves of the basic truths which Christians believe and by which we are called to live.

John was the son of Zebedee and Salome, probably the younger son. John was a cousin of Jesus on his mother's side. His parents appear to have been well-to-do, for his father, a fisherman, had *hired servants* (Mark 1:20); and Salome was one of the women who *provided for Jesus out of their means* (Luke 8:3; Mark 15:40).

John has often been identified as the unnamed disciple of John the Baptist, who with Andrew was directed by the Baptist to Jesus as the Lamb of God (John 1:35-37).

Jesus called upon James and John to leave their father and their fishing (Mark 1:19-20) and become his traveling companions. Jesus nicknamed the brothers *Boanerges, sons of thunder* (Mark 3:17), probably because they were high-spirited, impetuous Galileans. The zeal of the two brothers was undisciplined and sometimes misdirected (Luke 9:49, 54; Mark 10:37).

Along with his brother James and Peter, John was a member of the inner circle of disciples (Mark 5:37; 9:2; 14:33). He is not mentioned by name in the Fourth Gospel but he is almost certainly *the disciple whom Jesus loved*. This disciple lay close to the breast of Jesus at the Last Supper (John 13:23). He was entrusted with the care of Jesus' mother at the time of his death (John 19:26-27). John ran with Peter to the tomb on the first Easter morning. He was the first to see the full significance of the undisturbed grave-clothes with no body inside them (John 20:2, 8).

In early church history John is associated with Peter. The two of them were the focus of anti-Christian hostility (Acts 4:13; 5:33, 40; 8:14). John is described as a reputed "pillar" of the Jerusalem church at the time when Paul visited the city (Galatians 2:9).

62nd Book of the Bible
Book of 1 John
Assurance in Our Faith

Though simple in vocabulary and style, 1 John expresses some of the deepest truths of Scripture. Like 2 Peter and Jude, this book has a negative and a positive thrust. On the one hand it refutes false doctrine. At the same time John gives positive encouragement to his readers to walk in the knowledge of the truth.

The first epistle of John contains five chapters, 105 verses, and 2,523 words.

Situation

The Apostle John was probably working in Ephesus at the time he wrote his first letter. He was concerned about the inroads that the false doctrine of Gnosticism was making in the churches. Gnosticism held that knowledge is greater than love and that flesh is inherently evil. If flesh is inherently evil then Jesus must not have come in the flesh. He must have been a spirit being that materialized for a time. Gnostics believed that the human soul is not responsible for the deeds done by the body. This strange heresy was particularly strong in Asia Minor where John spent his last years. A date of about AD 90 is appropriate for this letter. This was during the reign of the Emperor Domitian.

Plan

The first letter of John is more like a sermon than a letter. It does not have the salutation and conclusion characteristic of most of the other New Testament epistles. The theme of the book is *fellowship in Christ*. Following a brief introduction the book unfolds in five thought units that correspond to the five chapters. The outline looks like this:

- ❖ **Introduction** (1:1-4)
- ❖ **Conditions for Fellowship** (1:5-10)
- ❖ **Conduct of Fellowship** (ch. 2)
- ❖ **Character of Fellowship** (ch. 3)
- ❖ **Cautions in Fellowship** (ch. 4)
- ❖ **Consequences of Fellowship** (ch. 5)

The only proper name in 1 John is that of *Cain, who slew his brother* (3:12). No locations are mentioned in the book. The book was probably written in Ephesus. For details about this city see under Ephesians. The destination of the letter was probably the churches of Asia Minor, a Roman province located in what is today western Turkey.

The style of John in this epistle is hammerlike. Certain ideas like light, love, life, truth, and righteousness come up again and again as John pounds home the truth. John also delights to place side by side opposite concepts: light and darkness, truth and falsehood, love and hatred, love of the world and love of the Father, Christ and antichrists, children of God and children of the devil, righteousness and sin, the Spirit of God and the spirit of antichrist, life and death.

Eternal Purpose

The immediate purpose of 1 John is to refute the false and destructive teaching of the Gnostics. The deeper purpose is to reassure believers of their standing with God.

In this epistle John attributes to God a quartet of wondrous qualities: God is light (1:5), love (4:8, 16), righteous (2:29), and the giver of eternal life (5:11-12).

In synopsis 1 John stresses that believers can have assurance of their standing before the Lord. Since God is light, life, and love, God's children must walk in the light, confess that Jesus has come in the flesh, and love their Christian brethren.

The basic truth that we can take from this book is that we can be confident of our standing with God.

On the practical side, 1 John sets forth fourfold evidence that we are living in fellowship with God: proper behavior (2:6; 3:9), the indwelling Spirit (3:24), faith in the Son of God (5:10-12), and the word of God (5:10-11).

Acclaim

The first epistle of John depicts the present ministry of Jesus (1:5-2:22). His blood continually cleanses the believer who confesses his sins. This book especially emphasizes the incarnation of Jesus and that he is the Christ (2:22; 4:2-3). He is the Son of God in the flesh (3:8). According to 5:6 Jesus came by water (his baptism) and blood (his death). He was the same person from the beginning to the end of his ministry.

Christ is the believer's hope. The Second Coming of Christ should be anticipated (2:28; 4:17). In that day the believer will be transformed (3:2). Those who look forward to the Second Coming purify themselves (3:3).

The portrait of Jesus that we will associate with 1 John is the ***Advocate with the Father*** (2:1).

Keys

The key chapter in 1 John is chapter 1. This is one of the central passages of the Bible that focuses on continued fellowship with God.

1, 2, & 3 John

The key verse in the book is this: *I write these things to you who believe in the name of the Son of God so that you may know that you have eternal life.* (5:13).

The key phrase is *little children* (9).

Key words include *light* (5), *life* (15), and *love* (33).

Special Features

Some of the interesting facts about 1 John that make this book unique in the sacred collection are these:

- ❖ John wrote his Gospel to prove the deity of Christ; his first epistle was written to prove Christ's humanity. Both teachings are equally vital to the Christian faith.
- ❖ 1 John has been called a family letter from the Father. It is perhaps the most intimate of the New Testament letters.
- ❖ The usual characteristics of a letter (salutation, address, greetings, benediction) are absent in this epistle.
- ❖ There are no quotations from the Old Testament in this book, only an allusion to one Old Testament incident.

HEAR

Here are some of the favorite lines from 1 John that may whet your appetite for detailed study of this book:

- ❖ *That which was from the beginning, which we have heard, which we have seen with our eyes, which we have looked at and our hands have touched — this we proclaim concerning the of the Word of life. . . . We proclaim to you what we have seen and heard, so that you also may have fellowship with us. And our fellowship is with the Father and with his Son, Jesus Christ* (1:1-3).
- ❖ *If we claim to be without sin, we deceive ourselves and the truth is not in us* (1:8).
- ❖ *If we confess our sins, he is faithful and just and will forgive us our sins and purify us from all unrighteousness* (1:9).
- ❖ *If anybody does sin, we have one who speaks to the Father in our defense — Jesus Christ the Righteous One* (2:1).

- *Even now many antichrists have come. This is how we know it is the last hour* (2:18).
- *Whoever acknowledges the Son has the Father also* (2:23).
- *How great is the love the Father has lavished on us, that we should be called children of God* (3:1).
- *We know that we have passed from death to life, because we love our brothers* (3:14).
- *There are three that testify: the Spirit, the water and the blood; and the three are in agreement* (5:7-8).

63rd Book of the Bible
Book of 2 John
Adherence to Christ

In the oldest manuscripts this postcard is attributed to John. The reference is to the Apostle John, the apostle of love. John battles the same error regarding the person of Christ in this epistle as he did in his first epistle.

The second epistle of John contains one chapter, thirteen verses, and 303 words.

Situation

The contents of 2 John indicate that this note was written about the same time as 1 John. Again a date of about AD 90 during the reign of the Emperor Domitian is appropriate. John probably is writing from Ephesus. The epistle is addressed to one he calls *the elect lady*. This may have been John's loving and respectful way of alluding to a local congregation, probably in Asia Minor. If this is correct, then *her children* (v. 1) would be a reference to the individual members of the church. It has been suggested that 1 John is a general message circulated among all the churches in Asia Minor, and 2 John is a personal letter to an individual church—a letter that accompanies their copy of 1 John. John also mentions *your elect sister* (v. 13)—probably a sister congregation.

Plan

Structural plan. Unlike 1 John, this letter has the introductory greeting and closing that were common to letters in that period. The theme of the letter is *abiding in Christ*. This theme is discussed in two paragraphs. The outline looks like this:

- ❖ **Introductory Greeting** (vv. 1-4)
- ❖ **Believer's Walk** (vv. 5-6)
- ❖ **Believer's Watch** (vv. 7-11)
- ❖ **Conclusion** (vv. 12-13)

There are no proper names or geographical references in 2 John.

Eternal Purpose

The immediate purpose of 2 John is to warn the elect lady about traveling missionaries who were really false teachers. The deeper purpose of this epistle is to instruct Christians that they are not to support false teachers in any manner.

In synopsis format 2 John looks like this: the apostle expresses joy that some walk according to the truth. Deceivers who denied that Jesus had come in the flesh had gone forth. These were to be shunned as false teachers.

Christians should take from this book the basic truth that we must not lend support of any sort to those who teach false doctrine.

Acclaim

Because of its size, 2 John does not have a great deal to contribute to Christology (teaching about Christ). The epistle does emphasize that one must confess Jesus Christ as having come in the flesh (v. 7) in order to have a relationship with God. Thus the true humanity of Christ is a vital Christian teaching. The portrait of Christ that we will associate with 1 John is the ***Son of the Father*** (v. 3).

Keys

The key verse in 2 John is this: *Anyone who runs ahead and does not continue in the teaching of Christ does not have God; whoever continues in the teaching has both the Father and the Son* (v. 9).

The key phrase in the book is *love one another* (1).

Key words include *love* (4) and *truth* (3).

Special Features

Some of the special features that set 2 John apart as unique in the Scriptures are these:

- ❖ This is the only book in the New Testament addressed to a lady (and she may not be an actual lady).
- ❖ John does not mention his own name or the name of "the lady." This omission may have been to prevent persecution by the Roman authorities.
- ❖ John's second letter reads a bit like a postscript to 1 John. The five chapters of the previous letter are here condensed into only thirteen verses.

HEAR

Aside from the key verse cited above, here are three other verses that are typical of John's second letter.

- ❖ *Many deceivers, who do not acknowledge Jesus Christ as coming in the flesh, have gone out into the world. Any such person is the deceiver and the antichrist* (v. 7).
- ❖ *If anyone comes to you and does not bring this teaching, do not take him into your house or welcome him* (v. 10).
- ❖ *This is love: that we walk in obedience to his commands* (v. 6).

64th Book of the Bible
Book of 3 John
Authority in Christ

In the oldest manuscripts of the New Testament the sixty-fourth book of the Bible is attributed to John. The writer is the Apostle John who calls himself *the elder*. This last letter of John in some respects is a counterbalance to his second letter. In 2 John the apostle dealt with the problem of extending hospitality to deceivers; in this letter he urges the extension of hospitality to believers. In 2 John truth is worth standing for; in 3 John truth is worth working for.

The third letter of John is organized into one chapter of fourteen verses and 299 words.

Situation

The three letters of John were all written at about the same time. A date of about AD 90 during the reign of the Emperor Domitian is appropriate.

John was writing to the beloved Gaius to commend him for his hospitality to missionaries and to warn Diotrephes about arrogance. The letter was probably carried by Demetrius for whom the apostle supplies a warm recommendation.

Plan

Structural plan. The theme of John's third letter is *contributing to the faith*. The letter is biographically organized with comments concerning three leaders in the church. The outline looks like this:

- ❖ **Introduction** (vv. 1-2)
- ❖ **To Gaius: His Generosity** (vv. 3-8)
- ❖ **About Diotrephes: His Arrogance** (vv. 9-11)
- ❖ **About Demetrius: His Testimony** (v. 12)
- ❖ **Conclusion** (vv. 13-14)

Biographical plan. As noted above, 3 John speaks to and about three church leaders. **Gaius** had extended hospitality to missionaries that had been sent forth by John. Three others by the name Gaius are mentioned in the New Testament: 1) Paul's traveling companion from Macedonia (Acts 19:29), 2) a believer in Derbe (Acts 20:4), and 3) Paul's host in Corinth (Romans 16:23; 1 Corinthians 1:14). John's Gaius is probably not to be identified with any of these other men of the same name. Clearly John had a deep affection for this man. Nothing further, however, is known about him.

Diotrephes (*di-aht'-rih-fees*) was so arrogant that he would not receive a letter from the Apostle John. This indicated that he did not accept the authority of the last living apostle of Christ. Nothing further is known about this man.

Demetrius (*dih-mee'-trih-uhs*) may have been the silversmith in Ephesus. He incited a riot directed against Paul because he feared that the apostle's preaching would threaten the sale of silver shrines of Diana (Artemas), the patron goddess of Ephesus (Acts 19:24-41). Demetrius probably was a guild master in charge of producing small silver copies of Diana's temple with a figure of the goddess inside. Although we cannot be sure, the Demetrius that John commends in this letter may be the same man who opposed Paul some three decades earlier. Demetrius had a threefold testimony that he had been faithful in the Lord. He had the witness of all men, the truth itself, and John. He may have carried 3 John from the writer to its original readers.

The third letter of John presumably was written from Ephesus; but no locations are mentioned by name.

Eternal Purpose

The immediate purpose of John's third letter is to respond to reports from traveling missionaries concerning the hospitality of Gaius and the hostility of Diotrephes. The deeper purpose of this letter is to exhort Christians to give tangible encouragement to faithful missionaries.

In synopsis format the letter looks like this: John commends Gaius and Demetrius for their stand for the truth. He condemns Diotrephes for his haughty spirit.

We should take from this little book the basic truth that we should extend hospitality to those who labor for the Lord.

John's third letter does not make any significant doctrinal contribution. The concept of truth, however, runs throughout this letter. On the practical side this letter emphasizes the virtues of proper behavior, prayer, faithful works in the church, submission to apostolic authority, and Christian integrity.

Acclaim

Christ is mentioned only indirectly in 3 John in verse 7—*It was for the sake of the Name that they went out*. The identical Greek construction is used in reference to the name of Jesus in Acts 5:40. Jesus is the Name above all names. It is in his name that Christians are to pray (John 14:13), evangelize (Acts 9:15), serve (Colossians 3:17), and baptize (Acts 2:38). By calling upon his name we are saved (Romans 10:13). Ultimately every knee will bow at his name (Phil 2:10). So the portrait of Jesus that we will take from this little book is **The Name**.

Keys

The key verse in 3 John is this: *I wrote to the church, but Diotrephes, who loves to be first, will have nothing to do with us* (v. 9).

The key phrase in the book is this: *receive the brothers* (1).

Key words include *beloved* (3) and *brothers* (3).

Special Features

Here are some facts that set 3 John apart within the sacred collection:
- ❖ 3 John is the smallest book in the Bible.
- ❖ The name of Jesus does not appear in 3 John.
- ❖ 3 John is the most personal of John's three letters.

HEAR

Aside from the key verse cited above, here are two passages in 3 John that are favorites of many.

- ❖ *I have no greater joy than to hear that my children are walking in the truth* (v. 4).
- ❖ *We ought therefore show hospitality to such men* [those who go out for the sake of the Name = missionaries] *so that we may work together for the truth* (v. 8).

Chapter Fourteen

PATMOS VISIONS
Book of Revelation

A brief glance at the final book in the Bible indicates that it is very different from any other book in the New Testament. This book is full of images, symbols, and word pictures. The technique used by the writer is what scholars call *apocalyptic*. Certain passages in Isaiah, Daniel, and Zechariah form the background of this type of literature. From about the second century BC to the third century AD this highly figurative style of writing was not uncommon. So Revelation has a form that was much more appreciated by the early Christians than it is by western Christians who prefer clear, concise, and chronological discourse.

Because of its complex imagery and symbolism, Revelation is the most difficult biblical book to interpret. Among believers there are five major systems of interpreting Revelation.

The *Preterists* see most of Revelation fulfilled in the days of the Roman Empire. For them the central event is the coming of Christ in judgment upon Jerusalem in AD 70.

Spiritual interpreters think the book depicts a struggle between good and evil through the ages. This approach is sometimes called the "idealistic" or "poetic" system.

The *continuous-historical* method of interpretation has Revelation depicting the major events (from a Christian point of view) from John's day to the end of the world. For example, they see pictures in this book of the breakup of the old Roman Empire, the rise of the papacy and Islam, the French Revolution, and the Protestant Reformation.

Futurists contend that most of the book of Revelation is still future. For them the book is all about the Great Tribulation—a supposed seven-year period following the Rapture of the church—just preceding the Second Coming of Christ.

The *parallelists* believe that Revelation depicts the events of the Christian age from the ascension of Christ to the Second Coming several times in parallel fashion. According to them we come to the end of time at several points in the book.

Most Christians do not make an issue over one's interpretation of the final book of the Bible. There are helpful insights from the interpreters of all of the schools of thought mentioned above. Probably there will never be unanimity of opinion about the meaning of the symbolism in the book, nor does there need to be. There are certain fundamental truths that stand out in the book regardless of which system of interpretation one might be inclined to accept.

66th Book of the Bible
Book of Revelation
Victory of Our Faith

In the earliest manuscripts of the New Testament the last book of the Bible is entitled *Apocalypse* or *Revelation of John*. Perhaps a better title comes from verse 1, *The Revelation of Jesus Christ*. The author of Revelation is John the apostle (1:1, 4, 9; 22:8).

Just as Genesis is the book of beginnings, Revelation is the book of endings or consummation. This book is all about demonstrating how God's program for his people will come to a happy ending in spite of all the fury of Satan and the world. Here the divine program of redemption comes to fruition. Here the holy name of God is vindicated before all creation.

Within the Christian community there are two very opposite extremes when it comes to this book. Some avoid Revelation, convinced that they cannot grasp its message. To them the book seems bizarre, scary, and totally mystifying. Others cannot talk enough about Revelation. To them the book is very simple when viewed through the lenses of some prophetic scheme put forth by a TV evangelist. These people would rather talk about what will happen to the world after the church has been Raptured, than to talk about what the church is supposed to be doing in the here and now. This overconfident approach can lead to unhealthy speculation, divisive dogmatism, and what has been called "newspaper exegesis," reading into the book whatever one reads in the morning paper.

The interpreter should steer a middle course between these two extremes. We should not avoid the book, for it is a rich mine of teaching about Christ and practical encouragement for troubled believers. We should seek to understand as much as possible while at the same time acknowledging that there is much we do not understand. We certainly should not separate ourselves from believers with a different view of the book. In the light of eternity we may find out that we were all wrong about the last book of the Bible!

Hundreds of symbolic objects and acts are depicted in Revelation. Many of these are either explained in the context or in some other part of the Bible. As we grow in our understanding of the previous books of Scripture, we will come to have better insight into the meaning of the last book of the Bible.

The Book of Revelation is organized into twenty-two chapters, 404 verses, and 12,000 words.

Situation

John presumably was ministering at Ephesus when the local Roman authorities banished him to the island of Patmos because of *the word of God and the testimony of Jesus* (Revelation 1:9). The exact date of this exile is uncertain. A date of about AD 96 would not be far off. At this time the churches were experiencing an intense persecution at the hands of the tyrant Domitian.

Plan

As noted above, Revelation as a whole falls into the category of apocalyptic literature. In apocalyptic literature there is widespread use of animal and number symbols. Apocalyptic literature envisions the end of time and the catastrophes that will introduce the golden age. The book, however, contains other types of literature as well such as letters, praise songs, and prophecies.

Structural plan. The theme of the book is the *successful struggle*. The book breaks down into four main divisions:

- ❖ **Introduction & Opening Visions** (ch. 1)
- ❖ **Desperate Struggle** (chs. 2–11)
- ❖ **Deeper Struggle** (chs. 12–20)
- ❖ **Final Vision & Conclusion** (chs. 21–22)

The opening vision depicts the glorious Christ as he walks among the lampstands, which John tells us symbolize the churches. In the second division the church is persecuted, protected, and avenged by judgments from God. This section features the opening of seven seals depicting the unfolding of events in the Christian age, and the sounding of seven trumpets warning of judgments to come. In the third division John reveals that behind the troubles of the church are powerful forces: the dragon (Satan), anti-Christian government (the beast from the sea), anti-Christian religion (the beast from the land), and Babylon (the secular world). Among other powerful figures this third division pictures the pouring out of bowls of judgment upon the kingdom of Satan, and the final eternal judgment at the great white throne. In the final division the focus is on the glorious City of God, the heavenly Jerusalem.

Biographical plan: Aside from John himself, no other Christian leader is mentioned in Revelation unless it is **Antipas** (*an'-tih-puhs*) (2:13). Antipas was killed in the city of Pergamum. Some writers think that Antipas is a symbol for Christian martyrs.

From the Old Testament John makes use of the name of *Jezebel*. This foreign princess married by King Ahab persecuted the prophets of God. John uses the name symbolically for a woman (or group) at Thyatira that was destroying true faith by encouraging idolatry and immorality. John mentions the key and root of *David*. Christ has the key of David (3:7) which symbolizes his authority over his kingdom. The root of David (5:5; 22:16) points to Jesus as the rightful ruler from the house of David. John refers to some at Pergamum who followed the doctrine of *Balaam* who taught *Balak* the king of Moab to sin.

In chapter 7 John references the names of the twelve tribes of Israel: *Judah, Reuben, Gad, Asher, Naphtali, Manasseh, Simeon, Levi, Issachar, Zebulun, Joseph,* and *Benjamin*. Some think John is speaking about the physical tribes of earthly Israel; others think these tribes symbolize the new Israel of God — the church — in its totality.

From the Book of Daniel John uses the name *Michael* the archangel. He is depicted fighting against the Dragon or Satan.

Geographical plan: The island called *Patmos* where John was in exile was fifty miles off the coast of western Turkey. It was a rocky island about ten miles long and five miles wide. A letter is addressed by Jesus through John to seven churches in the Roman province of Asia Minor (western Turkey): *Ephesus, Smyrna, Pergamum, Thyatira, Sardis, Philadelphia,* and *Laodicea*.

John speaks of the new *Jerusalem* (3:12; 21:2, 10) and *Mount Zion* (14:1), both of which may be symbols for God's kingdom here and hereafter. The great River *Euphrates* (9:14; 16:12) is referenced as the ancient boundary of the Promised Land. Some think *Babylon* (used 6×) is a symbolic name for Rome; others think Babylon is a symbol for Jerusalem or for the secular world. *Armageddon* is named as the place for the final showdown between the forces of good and evil. *Gog* and *Magog* (20:8) — two distant lands mentioned by Ezekiel — are named as the forces raised up by Satan to oppose God in the final showdown.

Eternal Purpose

The immediate purpose of the Book of Revelation is to encourage persecuted Christians to persevere with the assurance that their adversaries will soon be judged. The deeper purpose of the book is to assure believers of ultimate triumph in Christ.

A synopsis of Revelation looks like this: the ascended Christ addresses letters to seven churches. Then in a series of figures John sees the final doom of the wicked and the victory of the saints of God.

From this book Christians should take away the basic truth that we will overcome the world.

On a practical level John assures his readers that God sees their tears (7:17; 21:4), hears their prayers (8:3, 4), regards their death as precious (14:13; 20:4), assures them of final victory (15:2), and avenges their blood (6:9; 8:3).

The theme of *newness* is rich in Revelation. John speaks of a new heaven and earth (21:1), a new people (21:2-8), a new bride (21:9), a new home (21:10-21), a new temple (21:22), a new light (21:23-27), and a new Paradise (22:1-5).

Acclaim

Revelation is rich in titles for Jesus. Christ is the faithful witness, the firstborn from the dead, the ruler of the kings of the earth (1:5), and the First and Last (1:17). Jesus is he who lives (1:18), the Son of God (2:18), and the holy and true (3:7). Revelation depicts Christ as the Amen, the Faithful and true Witness, the Beginning of the creation of God (3:14), the Lion of the tribe of Judah, and the Root of David (5:5). He is the Lamb (5:6), the Faithful and True (19:11), the Word of God (19:13), King of kings and Lord of lords (19:16). Christ is called the Alpha and Omega (22:13), the Bright and Morning Star (22:16), and the Lord Jesus Christ (22:21).

The book begins with a vision of Christ's glory, wisdom, and power. It portrays his authority over the entire church (chs. 2-3). In chapter 5 Christ is the Lamb who was slain and declared worthy to open the book of judgment. In chapters 6-18 the righteous wrath of Christ is poured out upon the whole earth. In Revelation 19-20

Revelation

Christ returns in power to judge his enemies and to reign as the Lord over all. The book concludes with a picture of Christ ruling forever over the heavenly city in the presence of all who know him.

The Christ-portrait that we shall link with Revelation is this: **Crowned with Many Crowns** (19:12).

Keys

The key chapters in the Book of Revelation are 19–22. These chapters record the final destinies of the unbelieving world and the faithful church.

The key verse in the book is this: *Look, he is coming with the clouds, and every eye will see him* (1:7).

Key phrases in the book are *to the angel of the church* (7) and *I saw* (35).

The key word in Revelation is *seven* (54).

Special Features

Some of the facts that set Revelation apart within the sacred collection are these:

- ❖ Revelation is full of allusions to the Old Testament. Nearly three hundred of the approximately 404 verses have some connection to the Old Testament.
- ❖ Revelation is the only biblical book that begins by promising a special blessing on those who study it, and ends by promising a special curse on those who add to it or take away from it.
- ❖ In his Gospel John reached back into eternity farther than any other writer; in Revelation he stretches forward farther into eternity than any other writer.
- ❖ Revelation provides the happy ending to the tragic story unfolded in Genesis regarding man's fall from Paradise.
- ❖ This book lists more titles for Christ than any other book of the Bible.
- ❖ The numbers seven and twelve and multiples thereof are predominant in this book.

HEAR

Some of the favorite passages in Revelation that might provide a starting point for a study of this book:
- ❖ Opening verses (1:1-3).
- ❖ Our exalted Christ (1:4-6).
- ❖ Sealed book (5:1-10).
- ❖ Sealing of the saints (7:1-4). See also 14:1-5.
- ❖ Heavenly throng (7:9-17).
- ❖ Woman clothed with the sun (12:1-11).
- ❖ Thousand years (20:1-10).
- ❖ All things new (21:1-8).

Among the favorite lines in the Book of Revelation are the following.
- ❖ *God will wipe away every tear from their eyes (7:17).*
- ❖ *Look, he is coming with the clouds, and every eye will see him (1:7).*
- ❖ *So because you are lukewarm — neither hot nor cold — I am about to spit you out of my mouth (3:16).*
- ❖ *Blessed are the dead who die in the Lord (14:13)*
- ❖ *Then I saw a new heaven and a new earth, for the first heaven and the first earth had passed away (21:1).*
- ❖ *I am the Alpha and the Omega, the Beginning and the End (21:6).*
- ❖ *The Spirit and the bride say, "Come!" And let him who hears say, "Come!" Whoever is thirsty, let him come; and whoever wishes, let him take the free gift of the water of life (22:17).*

John's Writings Compared			
	His Gospel	**His Epistles**	**Revelation**
Emphasis:	Salvation	Sanctification	Glorification
Direction:	Looks Backward	Looks Within	Looks Forward
Christ View:	Prophet	Priest	King
Focal Point:	Cross	Church	Crown

Revelation

OTHER BOOKS BY THE AUTHOR

Available from College Press, Joplin, Mo. www.collegepress.com
  The Pentateuch, 1993, 534 pp.
  The Books of History, 1995, 747 pp.
  The Wisdom Literature and Psalms, 1996, 873 pp.
  The Major Prophets, 1992, 637 pp.
  The Minor Prophets, 1994, 653 pp.
  1 & 2 Samuel in "The College Press NIV Commentary," 2000. 541 pp.
  Bible History Made Simple, 2009, 180 pp.
  Old Testament Books Made Simple, 2009, 237 pp.

Also by this author:
  What the Bible Says about the Promised Messiah 1991, 522 pp.
  Biblical Protology, 2007, 530 pp.
  Postexilic Prophets, 2007, 268 pp.
  Daniel: A Christian Interpretation, 2008, 416 pp.
  Ezekiel: A Christian Interpretation, 2008, 468 pp.
  Jeremiah: A Christian Interpretation, 2008, 540 pp.

For articles and commentaries and other materials, check the author's web site: bibleprofessor.com